MW00514486

PERFECT JOY

PERFECT JOY

~ 30 Days with Francis of Assisi ~

KERRY WALTERS

Franciscan
MEDIA
Cincinnati, Ohio

Scripture passages have been taken from *New Revised Standard Version Bible*, copyright ©1989 by the Division of Christian Education of the National Council of the Churches of Christ in the U.S.A., and used by permission. All rights reserved.

Cover and book design by Mark Sullivan.
Cover image ©iStock | druvo

Library of Congress Cataloging-in-Publication Data
Names: Walters, Kerry S., author.
Title: Perfect joy : 30 days with Francis of Assisi / Kerry Walters.
Other titles: Finding perfect joy with St. Francis of Assisi
Description: Cincinnati, Ohio : Franciscan Media, 2016. | Originally published under title: Finding perfect joy with St. Francis of Assisi : 30 reflections : Ann Arbor, Mich. : Charis Books, c2002.
Identifiers: LCCN 2015049802 | ISBN 9781616369217 (alk. paper)
Subjects: LCSH: Francis, of Assisi, Saint, 1182-1226—Meditations. | Spiritual life—Catholic Church. | Joy—Religious aspects—Christianity.
Classification: LCC BX4700.F6 W25 2016 | DDC 248.4/82—dc23
LC record available at http://lccn.loc.gov/2015049802

ISBN 978-1-61636-921-7

Copyright ©2016, Kerry Walters. All rights reserved.
Published by Franciscan Media
28 W. Liberty St.
Cincinnati, OH 45202
www.FranciscanMedia.org

Printed in the United States of America.
Printed on acid-free paper.
16 17 18 19 20   5 4 3 2 1

For the wonderful people of Holy Spirit parish,
who bring me great joy.

CONTENTS

~ Looking for Happiness ~

TWENTY-FIVE CENTURIES AGO, ARISTOTLE WROTE A BOOK CALLED *Nicomachean Ethics*, in which he concluded that the ultimate goal of human beings is and ought to be happiness. Aristotle's book became a classic long ago. But when you think about it, its thesis is rather commonplace. When we honestly examine our lives, we quickly realize that what we want is to be happy. What sane person wouldn't? So we scarcely need an ancient Greek philosopher to tell us what we already know.

What isn't so obvious is *how* to be happy. There are any number of answers out there competing for our attention. The advertising industry, for example, spends billions of dollars annually to tell us that true happiness lies in buying this or that product. Pop psychologists assure us that happiness consists in getting in touch with our primordial self, looking out for number one, or learning how to be intimate. (It all depends on which psychologist you read.)

Speaking of intimacy, popular films and novels imply that we need lots of sex to be happy. And let's not forget money, power, fame, and social influence: These are all touted by various prophets as surefire keys to the kingdom of happiness.

We all want to be happy, but we don't quite know how to go about it. And therein lies the problem, as old Aristotle recognized full well. His diagnosis was that our confusion arises because we too frequently confuse happiness with pleasure. There's obviously a connection between the two, but they're not identical.

Pleasures, which are typically responses to external stimuli, tend to be short-lived and sporadic. Moreover, even though immediate pleasurable sensations feel good, they may, in fact, be harmful to our well-being. The pleasurable rush of a cigarette is an obvious example of a harmful pleasure.

Happiness, on the other hand, is more of an abiding inner state than a transient response to an external stimulus. It can feel good at times, but because happiness isn't identical to pleasure, it's perfectly possible to be happy even while enduring pain. Additionally, genuine happiness isn't deceptive in the way pleasure can be. Happiness is never harmful, precisely because it's the consequence of living a fulfilled, enriched life. When a person achieves the possibilities essential to his or her nature—when a person becomes a human in the fullest sense of the word—then happiness is attained.

If Aristotle is right about this distinction between pleasure and happiness—and I think he is—it follows that many of us may be selling our chance for happiness short by settling for mere pleasure. Lots of pleasures—perhaps most pleasures—are innocent enough. But they can't give us the happiness we crave, even if we add thousands and thousands of them together. If we're unhappy, then, it's not because happiness is out of our reach; it's because we simply haven't stretched as high as we could and should.

HAPPINESS AS PERFECT JOY

Francis of Assisi was someone who stretched as high as he could, and in doing so he found genuine happiness, or what he liked to call "perfect joy." Like so many of us, Francis began his search in some confusion, mistaking transient pleasures for the joy he desired. It took him a few years of steadily growing dissatisfaction to figure out where he'd gone wrong. Then, with God's help, he discovered what Aristotle already knew centuries earlier: that true happiness, perfect joy, is possible only when we live up to our innate potentiality and become fully human.

Aristotle, philosopher that he was, thought what made us fully human was our use of reason. But Francis dug deeper, arriving at the far richer conclusion that fulfillment lay in the heartfelt recognition that we're made in the image of the living God and that our final purpose in life is to conform reason and will, body and soul, to that image. Perfect joy, in other words, comes when we model ourselves after Christ, the new human, the second Adam, the perfect example of what we can and should be. This is our destiny. This is what we were made for.

Francis spent his entire adult life striving for this conformity to Christ. Fortunately for us, each stage along his way was chronicled in great detail by his contemporaries. Taken together, these accounts give us a marvelously insightful record of what it means to travel the path to God, human fulfillment, and perfect joy. They allow us to embrace Francis as our spiritual director and follow in his footsteps as best we can so that we might find for ourselves what he found.

Even so, we need to begin our journey with eyes wide open, because the path Francis trod isn't always a pleasant one. Remember: True happiness, perfect joy, isn't identical with pleasure. If we choose Francis as a spiritual director, we must make an effort to take what he says seriously, even when it goes against the grain.

G.K. Chesterton once wisely wrote that people who admire Francis often do so because they fixate on those aspects of his life that please them while ignoring the ones they find unsettling or even repugnant. This obviously won't do. Francis must be taken as he is. Scrubbing away anything about him that we find distasteful might leave us with a charming (and unthreatening) garden statue. But garden statues make poor spiritual directors.

One of the most disconcerting features of the real Francis—and hence of his message to us today—is his uncompromising commitment to Christ. Let's be honest: Many of us are what C.S. Lewis liked to call "whiskey-and-soda Christians." We prefer our Christianity watered down. Taken straight, it's simply too strong for our weak stomachs. So we sidestep all the scriptural injunctions calling us to make radical changes in our lifestyles—loving our enemies, turning the other cheek, pooling possessions for the common good, voluntary poverty, sacrificing ourselves for the sake of others. We either ignore passages like these altogether or interpret them to mean something much less radical than Christ intended.

But Francis took Christ's teaching seriously. He was too honest to read Scripture selectively and too unsophisticated to spin elaborate no-risk interpretations of it. Instead, he championed the radical notion that Christ meant what he said when he spoke of love and poverty and sacrifice. To presume otherwise is to conclude that Christ was in the strange habit of always saying one thing but meaning something quite different.

So Francis's spiritual journey became the lifelong conversion of himself to Christ. As St. Paul might have said, Francis wished to "put on" Christ while simultaneously shucking off his old self, the Francis-centered ego (see Romans 13:14). To that end, he preached and practiced the three virtues he saw as most central to Christ's life and teaching: poverty, simplicity, and humility.

Francis told his followers that when they wed Lady Poverty, they freed their bodies from the enslavement to possessions that breeds violence. When they embraced Holy Simplicity, they liberated their minds and hearts from internal vanities and ambitions that distracted them from God. And when they embraced Gracious Humility, they released their spirit to acknowledge gratefully its utter dependence on the Creator of the universe.

On a grander scale, poverty, simplicity, and humility free us to love because they destroy fear, the single greatest impediment to love. And when we learn to love with something like the love God has for creation, we arrive at the end for which we are made. We grow into our Godlikeness. We live fully and richly.

We also live *joyfully*. Poverty, as Francis and his followers discovered, is frequently quite unpleasant; no one likes to go hungry or thirsty or unsheltered from the weather. Simplicity and humility are likewise often painful. It's so much easier to read theology than to live the Gospel, or to strike back than to turn the other cheek. But these unpleasantries are just transient reactions ultimately unable to override the deep happiness or perfect joy that comes when we fulfill our potentiality as loving images of God.

This is the incredible message that Francis brought to his world—a world, much like our own, sunk in forgetfulness and indifference, a world that preferred its Christianity watered down. His message, which was really Christ's message, revitalized the spiritual climate of his day. So many persons (especially idealistic younger ones) opened their hearts to what Francis had to say that he formed the secular Third Order for them so that they might continue their lives in the "ordinary" world while striving to prove worthy of perfect joy.

Mirroring Perfection

One of the most popular intellectual fashions of the Middle Ages was what might be called "mirror theology." This way of thinking, first popularized by St. Augustine in the fifth century, reasoned that even though we can never encounter God face-to-face during this life, we can see reflections of divine perfection in the world if we know how to look for them. Creation, in other words, is a mirror of the Creator; the masterpiece carries the distinctive signature of the artist. Thus God's guiding hand can be inferred from the uniform laws of nature, God's beauty from natural splendor, and God's goodness from human acts of loving compassion. Each of these reflects (although necessarily distorts as well, because reflections are one-dimensional) the perfection of God.

A Christian believes that God was incarnate in Jesus the Christ, who suffered and died a cruel and horrible death for the sake of love. Consequently, one of mirror theology's primary claims was that God is also discernible in the faces of suffering human beings. The beggar on the street, the leper in the hospital, the criminal, the dying patient, the abused child: each of these are reflections of the suffering Christ, each mirrors of the incarnate God.

Finally, mirror theology taught that especially holy men and women could be clear and shining mirrors reflecting the glory of God. Their very lives, conformed as they are to Christ's life, make Christ's face present to those of us who observe their actions or read about their journeys. Through them, God comes a little closer.

Even during his own lifetime, people considered Francis a *speculum perfectionis*, or a "mirror of perfection." Thomas of Celano, his first biographer, tells us that this was because Francis "was always occupied with Jesus; Jesus he bore in his heart, Jesus in his mouth, Jesus in his ears, Jesus in his eyes, Jesus in his hands, Jesus in the rest of his members." To watch Francis or listen to his words was to watch and heed the Christ shining through him.

This is undoubtedly the primary reason so many people flocked to the poor little man of God, eager to follow him in poverty, simplicity, and humility. Yet, Francis never forgot that he was but a mirror, and he refused to let others overlook that fact, either. He sometimes referred to himself as an icon (which, of course, is a sort of spiritual mirror or window). An icon is venerated not because of its wood and paint and lacquer, which after all are commonplace materials, but because an artisan has worked the wood and paint in such a way as to reveal Jesus, Mary, or one of the saints or angels.

Francis the icon, Francis the mirror, still inspires us today. When we reflect prayerfully on his life and teachings, we discern the presence of Christ and find ourselves moved to cleave to that presence. More specifically, Francis is a *speculum perfectionis* for us in at least three ways.

First, his life mirrors for us the human heart's longing for God. Francis's life can be seen as an archetypal spiritual pilgrimage in which the searching soul progresses from initial confusion and self-absorption to clarity and God-absorption. In following the various spiritual stages he traversed, we learn something about our own journey.

Second, Francis is a mirror that reflects what it means to be a fully developed human being. As we've already noted, our greatest gift is the innate potential to grow into Godlikeness. As individuals, we can reject this splendid destiny and doom ourselves to forlorn exile, or we can embrace the end for which we were made and strive to live up to it. Francis chose the second alternative, and when we gaze into his face, we see a reflection of both what we now are and what we might become.

Third, Francis is a mirror of what it means to experience perfect joy. For true happiness is that state of being in which an individual comes into his or her own by conforming to the living God. Put another way, perfect joy is attained when our will and actions are so aligned to God's that we, like our good brother Francis, become mirrors of perfection. Merely saying this runs the risk of making it sound platitudinous or impossibly unattainable, but Francis's life shows us that it's an entirely realizable ideal. All one need do is dare.

THIRTY DAYS WITH FRANCIS

This little book is itself a mirror of sorts: a mirror that reflects Francis, but also a mirror into which you, the reader, can gaze and possibly discern truths about yourself. Thirty episodes from Francis's life are offered here as catalysts for prayerful meditation. Taken together, they chart the course of his spiritual journey from confusion and unhappiness to perfect joy and fulfillment in God.

In keeping with the spirit of mirror theology, each chapter begins with a selection of Francis's own words immediately followed by accounts of Francis written by his contemporaries and near-contemporaries or by one of his twentieth-century admirers. These excerpts, many of which are reminiscent of parables, not only express each chapter's theme, but also offer excellent opportunities for prayerful meditation because they serve as mirrors that reflect both who Francis was and what we can become. Then comes a reflection in which I share some thoughts about the spiritual journey sparked by the mirror excerpts. Finally, each chapter concludes with questions for reflection and a quotation to meditate on from either Scripture or a spiritual author, both of which are intended to encourage reflection. Specific references for all the quotations may be found at the end.

This book can, of course, be read straight through. But it might be helpful to use it as the foundation for a thirty-day at-home retreat, meditating on one chapter a day. Francis's followers were always amazed at how his words filled their hearts with an unbearable longing for the perfect joy of God, prodding them to become better persons than they were before they gazed into the mirror of his life. Those of us today who heed Francis will discover the same.

1182: Francis is born in Assisi, late summer or early fall, to Pietro and Pica di Bernardone.

1202: After a few years of adolescent revelry, Francis decides to devote himself to knighthood and chivalry. He enlists in the war between Perugia and Assisi, fights, and is captured in the Battle of Collestrada. Then he remains a prisoner of war until ransomed by Pietro a year later.

1204: Upon returning home from Perugia's prison, Francis suffers a long illness. On his recovery, he sets out for war in Apulia but returns the next day when he has an unsettling dream. The dream is generally seen as the beginning of his conversion.

1205: Following about a year of intense soul searching, Francis hears the crucifix in the broken-down chapel of San Damiano order him to "repair the church."

1206: Francis strips himself naked in Assisi's square and declares that henceforth God is his only father. He spends the rest of the year rebuilding San Damiano and nursing lepers, as well as repairing two other local chapels. One of them, la Portiuncula, will become the home base of his future religious order.

1208: Francis discovers his vocation to poverty and begins preaching. His first followers join him.

1209: Francis travels to Rome to seek Pope Innocent III's approval for the Rule he's written for himself and his brothers.

1210: The Third Order is founded.

1211: Francis travels to the Middle East (Dalmatia) for the first time.

1212: Clare is received into the Order.

1217: Francis steps down as leader of the Order to devote himself to prayer, preaching, and good works.

1219: Francis returns to the Middle East and preaches to the sultan.

1220: Francis probably visits the Holy Land. He returns to Italy to discover that the Order, under the guidance of Brother Elias, is moving away from its original devotion to poverty, simplicity, and humility.

1223: Francis revises the Order's Rule, which is approved by Pope Honorius III.

1224: During a vigil at LaVerna, Francis receives the stigmata, probably on September 14.

1225: Quite ill at San Damiano, Francis composes his "Canticle of Brother Sun."

1226: After months of intense suffering, Francis returns to la Portiuncula, the place he loves most on earth, and dies on October 3.

CHAPTER ONE

~ Betwixt and Between ~

FRANCIS'S WORDS

Try to realize the dignity God has conferred on you. He created
and formed your body in the image of his beloved Son, and your
soul in his own likeness.

—*Admonitions*

MIRROR

About my mother and father, Brother Leo. The two of them
have been wrestling inside me for ages. This struggle has lasted
my whole life…. They may take on different names—God and
Satan, spirit and flesh, good and bad, light and darkness—but
they always remain my mother and father. My father cries within
me: "Earn money, get rich, use your gold to buy a coat of arms,
become a nobleman. Only the rich and the nobility deserve to
live in the world. Don't be good; once good, you're finished!" …
And my mother, her voice trembling within me, says to me softly,
fearfully, lest my father hear her: "Be good, dear Francis, and you
shall have my blessing. You must love the poor, the humble, the
oppressed."

—Nikos Kazantzakis, *Saint Francis*

THE SPIRITUAL JOURNEY WE'RE CALLED TO MAKE IS POSSIBLE only
because each one of us has the capacity for movement. This obser-
vation may strike you as boringly obvious. After all, to go on a

journey means to travel from point A to point B. So of course movement is involved!

Yet the apparent obviousness of the statement slips away when we ask this question: How is it that we're capable of spiritual movement in the first place? Muscles, nerve firings, and skeletal structure allow us to move physically. But what's the source of soul locomotion?

C.S. Lewis provides us with an intriguing answer. He says that soul locomotion can be chalked up to the fact that we're spiritually amphibious creatures. We dwell in two different (although overlapping) worlds. We're physical creatures whose feet are firmly planted on the earth, but we're also spiritual ones who yearn to leap toward heaven.

As St. Gregory of Nazianzus noted centuries ago, our earthly characters attract us to earthly existence. But being made as we are by God, we carry in our hearts a yearning for something beyond.

Because of our amphibious nature, we're subject to what Lewis calls the "law of oscillation": Sometimes we veer or oscillate toward our physical nature, sometimes toward our spiritual one. Like pendulums, we swing between the two poles of existence. This back-and-forth rhythm can be quite painful at times, making us feel as if we're torn between the devil and the deep blue sea. How to reconcile our lusty desire for the things of the earth with our heart's yearning for heaven?

Yet, distressing as this restlessness is, it's also a great blessing because it is the source of soul locomotion. Our double nature keeps us on the move, never in one place for very long, continuously propelled by desires that clash and clamor for reconciliation, ceaselessly nudging us closer and closer to where we need to go: God. As St. Augustine famously proclaimed at the beginning of his *Confessions*, "Thou hast formed us for thyself, and our hearts are restless till they find their rest in thee."

It's a wonderful gift, this never-ceasing oscillation. Granted, at times it might be more comfortable to be an object like a stone or a toothbrush. Objects aren't amphibious. They don't sway back and forth. They have no capacity for spiritual movement and so don't feel the pain of conflicting desires.

But they also have no potential for greatness, for transcendence, for spiritual insight. Who of us, even in our most painful moments, would really trade places with an inanimate, soulless thing? When one weighs all the pros and cons, discomfort seems a small price to pay for the journey toward God.

St. Francis knew about the law of oscillation centuries before C.S. Lewis. He experienced it for himself. The back-and-forth struggle he waged with his own amphibious nature is often symbolized by the different personalities of his parents.

His father, the worldly merchant Pietro di Bernardone, represents the selfishly earthy side of Francis; his mother, Pica, the spiritually self-giving side. In Francis, as in each of us, these two temperamental tendencies warily circled one another and frequently battled, causing him much suffering. But the tumult of their clashes progressively prodded him toward a richer understanding of who he was and where he wanted—where he *needed*—to go.

The ultimate goal of the journey, as Francis finally realized, is not to focus on one side of our amphibious nature at the expense of the other, but to reconcile the two into an integrated and harmonious whole. Demons and angels—our darkest impulses and our noblest aspirations—clash in our deepest core. We advance not by slaying the demons, but by accepting them for what they are, pitying them, and slowly, painstakingly converting them, until both of our sides harmonize as notes in a living hymn.

FOR REFLECTION

At what point on the pendulum's arc are you right now? Do you feel you have any control over which way you swing, or do you worry that the back-and-forth movement is simply something that happens to you?

MEDITATION

Within every heart abide angels and demons; a volcanic passion shows itself in every human action; life and death instincts abound within every person; desires to reach out, desires of communion with others and of self-giving live alongside the urges of selfishness, of rejection, of meanness. This is especially true of the lives of the saints. If they are saints, it is because they sense all of this not as destructive; but rather, overcoming them by facing them, checking and channeling them toward the good.

—Leonardo Boff, *Francis of Assisi: A Model for Human Liberation*

CHAPTER TWO

~ Desperate Revelry ~

FRANCIS'S WORDS

All the talent and ability, all the learning and wisdom which [the frenetically worldly person] thought his own, are taken away from him.

—*Letter to the Faithful*

MIRROR

Francis grew up quick and clever, and he followed in his father Pietro's footsteps by becoming a merchant. In business, however, he was very different from Pietro, being far more high-spirited and open-handed. He was also intent on games and songs; and day and night he roamed about the city of Assisi with companions of his own age. He was a spendthrift, and all that he earned went into eating and carousing with his friends.

—*The Legend of the Three Companions*

THE EASIEST THING IN THE WORLD TO DO IS TO MISUNDERSTAND our innate amphibious restlessness. We feel a nagging sense of incompleteness and dissatisfaction. But instead of recognizing it as a summons from God, we too often write it off as nothing more than a psychological itch that can be scratched by frenetic worldly activity.

Some of us, like Pietro di Bernardone, try to assuage our uneasiness through the pursuit of wealth and prestige. Others fervently commit themselves to a political or social cause. Still others run after love affairs. There are many different escape mechanisms. Anything that occupies time and gives the illusion of actually doing something will suffice—at least for the short run.

Before his conversion, Francis's favorite strategy for coping with his own restlessness was revelry. By all accounts he was an indifferent merchant, so his father's addiction to business didn't suit him. What did suit him was song and dance and drink and moonlit escapades.

Night after night Francis and his youthful boon companions roamed the backstreets of Assisi looking for adventure. Francis usually played the host, throwing away fistfuls of Pietro's hard-earned silver on various entertainments. The partying would continue until dawn. Then Francis would creep back to his home to fall wearily on his bed, exhausted in both body and spirit, only to commence again the next night. Neither wine nor music eased the ache in his soul.

Francis's error lay in searching for fulfillment in the wrong place. He presumed that he could satisfy his restlessness exclusively with things of the world, when what he also yearned for were things of the spirit. Wine and song and romance aren't evil. They're God's gifts to us and, like all of creation, are causes for celebration. But the value they possess is a borrowed one. The pleasure we experience from them is genuine enough, but only a dim reflection of the ultimate joy that originates with God, the joy for which our hearts truly pine. Anything less than this perfect joy is bound to be unsatisfying.

There's a law of diminishing returns at work when it comes to merrymaking. Because wine and song fail to satisfy us completely, we ratchet up our pursuit of them under the presumption that higher levels of intensity will bring proportionate satisfaction. This approach, of course, is folly.

Pleasures that by their very nature are incapable of ultimately fulfilling us won't do so merely because we chase after them in a frenzy. On the contrary, revelry driven by desperation loses whatever innocence it might have had, becoming a self-destroying addiction. Yet, unhappily, this is the situation most revelers eventually find themselves in. It's certainly the bog that threatened to swallow Francis.

The irony here is that our frenetic pursuit of fun and frolic often springs from a disguised but deep-seated boredom. Boredom is the psychological correlate of a chronic lack of direction or purpose. People who party as the young Francis did frequently do so because they're awash in an ocean of ennui and desperately in need of something to distract them.

The bored person glimpses no wonder in the world, no splendor in the sheer act of being. Everything appears drab and dusty and uninteresting, and this grimy coating can only be cut through by increasing bouts of revelry. What a sad, self-defeating existence. Unless we can find a way to face our boredom squarely and, in so doing, recognize that the meaning we seek isn't to be found solely in the world, we join the ranks of those trapped in not-so-quiet desperation.

As C.S. Lewis said, we humans are amphibians. That means we must occupy *both* spheres of reality, the physical *and* the spiritual, if we're to flourish. If we don't, even the dim worldly pleasures to which we cling will molder away to dust and ashes.

FOR REFLECTION

How do you typically respond to your own moments of boredom? Are you a reveler, like the youthful Francis, or do you scratch your itch in other ways?

MEDITATION

The world is eaten up by boredom. To perceive this needs a little preliminary thought: you can't see it all at once. It is like dust. You go about and never notice, you breathe it in, you eat and drink it. It is sifted so fine, it doesn't even grit on your teeth. But stand still for an instant and there it is, coating your face and hands. To shake off this drizzle of ashes you must be forever on the go. And so people are always "on the go."

—Georges Bernanos, *The Diary of a Country Priest*

CHAPTER THREE

~ A False Start ~

FRANCIS'S WORDS

Do not look at the life without,
for that of the Spirit is better.

—The Canticle of Exhortation

MIRROR

Francis was soon shown in a vision a splendid palace in which he saw various military apparatus and a most beautiful bride. In the dream Francis was called by name and enticed by the promise of all these things. He attempted, therefore, to go to Apulia to win knighthood; and after he had made the necessary preparations in a lavish manner, he hurried on to gain that degree of military honors. A carnal spirit prompted him to make a carnal interpretation of the dream he had had, while a far more glorious interpretation lay hidden in the treasures of God's wisdom.

—Thomas of Celano, *Second Life of Francis*

ONE OF THE PROBLEMS WITH BOREDOM-DRIVEN REVELRY IS THAT it dulls our spiritual palates. Instead of opening ourselves to the exciting possibility of brand new spiritual foods, we mechanically stick with our old unsatisfying ones out of habit. Our jaded senses lock us into a world of increasingly dull flavors, and our spiritual taste buds are simply too exhausted to notice it.

Francis is a case in point. Like so many merrymakers, he finally reached the saturation point. The law of diminishing returns kicked in with a vengeance and the game was up: He could find neither goblet deep enough nor joke witty enough to sate his bored restlessness. The walls began to close in on him. His fellow revelers noticed that he was often strangely absent in the midst of their frolicking.

But Francis was fortunate. Unlike so many other persons who find themselves similarly trapped in a futureless prison of their own making, he caught a glimpse of a brighter world. It dawned on him that perhaps humans are intended for a nobler destiny than desperate revelry. And what better destiny for a prosperous young man in the thirteenth century than knighthood?

Francis always had a soft spot for tales of knightly chivalry and derring-do. Even after his conversion, he liked to refer to his followers as chevaliers of the Round Table. So when he dreamt of the armor-filled palace, it was only natural that he should take it as a portent of military glory.

Suddenly a way out of his directionless boredom opened before him: Sir Francis, gallant knight. In a flash he rejected his devil-may-care revelry for the more purposeful calling of knightly service. After wheedling expensive and flashy armor from Pietro (whose own vanity was probably tickled at the prospect of a military hero in the family), Francis set out for Apulia to win his spurs.

Thomas of Celano tells us that Francis's military ambition was a false start, that he misread the dream, giving a "carnal interpretation" to that which was spiritual. The dream was a breaking-in of fresh, previously unimagined opportunity. Sadly, Francis the erstwhile reveler, bored with his existence yet unable as yet to liberate himself from its narrowness, interpreted it in prosaic, worldly terms.

God called his name and spoke to his heart. But Francis's spiritual hearing was too dull to appreciate the true meaning of the call. His hope for a knightly future was a false start.

Many of us suffer from a similar kind of jadedness that prompts us to make our own false starts. We reach a point in life where our accustomed spiritual fast foods no longer satisfy and we look around for a meatier diet, a higher calling to which we can devote ourselves. Few of us become knights in this day and age. Instead, we latch onto a charity, or pledge ourselves to some political "ism," or enlist under the banner of the latest social crusade.

We might even do so in an admirably tireless way, dedicating our time and energy to the cause we've picked. But for all that, we could be selling ourselves short. What we take to be a higher calling may turn out to be not so terribly high after all, merely another strategy to fill time and escape from boredom. The narcotic of revelry is replaced with the narcotic of nobility.

One of the most common ways of tricking ourselves into thinking that we're pursuing a higher calling is in service to the Church. (By the way, this really isn't all that different from Francis's mistake. In the thirteenth century, knighthood was seen as a holy calling.) We feel within us a call to be better Christians and to serve God in a more intentional and dedicated way.

As Francis will tell us in future chapters, the only way to do this is to take Jesus's message so seriously that we actually live it. But our jaded spiritual palates are often unable to appreciate genuinely new foods, and we mistakenly assume that our obligations as Christians are fulfilled—that we're pursuing a higher calling—if we merely attend church more regularly, toss a few more bucks into the collection plate, or join a church committee. We might even be admired as wonderfully dedicated by our fellow parishioners.

But for all that, we could be mediocre Christians unable to fathom the meaning of our call. Outward piety doesn't make a Christian any more than a fine suit of armor makes a knight.

FOR REFLECTION

Do you serve a higher calling? Have you enlisted in its service from a genuinely interior urging, or is it just another strategy for escaping boredom?

MEDITATION

We are half-hearted creatures, fooling about with drink and sex and ambition when infinite joy is offered us, like an ignorant child who wants to go on making mud pies in a slum because he cannot imagine what is meant by the offer of a holiday at sea. We are far too easily pleased.

—C.S. Lewis, *The Weight of Glory*

CHAPTER FOUR

~ Whom Do You Serve? ~

FRANCIS'S WORDS

We must renounce self and bring our lower nature into subjection under the yoke of obedience.

—Letter to All the Faithful

MIRROR

While he was sleeping one night, someone addressed him a second time in a vision and questioned him solicitously as to whither he intended to go. When he had told his purpose to him who was asking and said that he was going to Apulia to fight, he was asked earnestly who could do better for him, the servant or the Lord. And Francis said: "The Lord." The other answered: "Why then are you seeking the servant in place of the Lord?"

—Thomas of Celano, Second Life of Francis

WE'VE SEEN THAT REVELRY AND NOBLE AMBITION ARE TWO WAYS in which bored folks try to keep themselves occupied. As such, they're defense strategies whose main purpose is to protect us from the awful realization that something incredibly important is missing from our lives. Not all fun is desperate revelry, nor is all ambition falsely noble. Genuine laughter and cheerful companionship are wonderful gifts, and urges toward higher callings can certainly be legitimate and well worth pursuing. The difficulty is learning how to distinguish between sheep and goats.

So what's the litmus test for doing so?

Thomas of Celano's story about Francis's second dream provides us with as good a one as we could desire.

A few days into his journey to Apulia, Francis the would-be knight has another dream. The first dream was enticing; this one is disturbing. It asks Francis a question he's never considered before: Whom are you really seeking?

As is the case with many dreams, the question is cloaked in a riddle: Who is more important, the servant or the Lord? In giving the predictably appropriate response that the Lord is more important, Francis suddenly realizes that he's placed the servant above the Lord. This insight is a turning point in his life.

The dream is so important because it's the distasteful tangy catalyst that reawakens Francis's spiritual palate. It forces him to admit that his priorities have been upside down, that he's misguidedly devoted himself to the insubstantial (the servant) while all but ignoring the essential (the Lord). And how has he done this? By seeking himself first and foremost.

In his youthful partying days, his only priority was sensual gratification. In his subsequent higher-calling days, his only priority was ego-gratification, the desire to feel good about himself because of his pursuit of a noble ambition. But such priorities clearly show that Francis took himself as the only lord worth serving.

The youthful Francis was an idolater, and the god he worshipped was himself. Like Francis, too many of us are self-worshippers, seeking our own gratification or our own advancement before everything else. We do this under the presumption that nothing's more important in the whole world than our own lives, wants, hopes, and dreams. Why would we think otherwise? The culture in which we dwell endlessly encourages us to seek out and serve Numero Uno.

But the restlessness and boredom from which we suffer can never be calmed by this kind of idolatry. The self is just too puny to serve as a god. The deep-down restlessness we experience inexorably points beyond the self to something greater, to an object truly worthy of our desire and veneration. This object, of course, is God, the supreme ground of our being, the ultimate foundation of our existence—the Lord, not the servant. Until we consciously come to accept this reality, we run around in circles, fruitlessly spinning our wheels in the service of ego.

The curious thing is that we have known this all along, even if we haven't articulated it to ourselves. The heart is frequently wiser than the head and will point us in the right direction—toward God—if we but follow its lead. We are made for God, and this means that despite our amphibious oscillation we're spiritually hardwired to gravitate toward God in the end. Every cell in our body pulsates with this longing. As the twentieth-century theologian Karl Rahner says, this deep-seated but generally unconscious awareness of God serves as the horizon of our experience, the ever-present backdrop against which we read reality.

For the medieval mind, great spiritual truths were frequently conveyed by God through dreams. Today, most of us no longer believe that dreams are divine messages. Instead, we think of them as exclusively psychological phenomena.

But perhaps we ought not to rush to judgment. If an unspoken knowledge of God lies buried in our heart, dreams may well be one way that the knowledge works its way to the surface. What the stubborn conscious mind refuses to acknowledge wells up from the subconscious when our defenses are dropped during sleep.

Such a thing, at any rate, happened to Francis so many centuries ago when his heart reminded him that he was servant and not master. At that turning point, he finally understood that human fulfillment lies in subordination to the one who is always and everywhere greater than the self. Henceforth, he would be a knight of Christ.

FOR REFLECTION
Have you consciously placed yourself under the yoke of service, or do you secretly think of yourself as the master? Are you, in other words, a self-worshipper?

MEDITATION
Then Jesus told his disciples, "If any want to become my followers, let them deny themselves and take up their cross and follow me. For those who want to save their life will lose it, and those who lose their life for my sake will find it. For what will it profit them if they gain the whole world but forfeit their life? Or what will they give in return for their life?"

—Matthew 16:24–26

CHAPTER FIVE

~ Lord as Leper ~

FRANCIS'S WORDS

When I was in sin, the sight of lepers nauseated me beyond measure; but then God himself led me into their company, and I had pity on them. When I had once become acquainted with them, what had previously nauseated me became a source of spiritual and physical consolation for me.

—The Testament

MIRROR

Among all the unhappy spectacles of the world Francis naturally abhorred lepers; but one day he met a leper while he was riding near Assisi. Though the leper caused him no small disgust and horror, nevertheless, lest like a transgressor of a commandment he should break his given word, he got off the horse and prepared to kiss the leper. But when the leper put out his hand as though to receive something, he received money along with a kiss. And immediately mounting his horse, Francis looked here and there about him; but though the plain lay open and clear on all sides, and there were no obstacles about, he could not see the leper anywhere.

—Thomas of Celano, Second Life of Francis

WE AWAKEN ONE DAY FROM A SPIRITUAL COMA TO REALIZE that we're the servant rather than the lord. This is an intensely liberating moment, but it doesn't necessarily sweep away all our misperceptions about either God or the nature of our inner restlessness. We may begin to look for a Lord who simply doesn't exist outside of our imagination.

The Anglican priest J.B. Phillips once wrote a book entitled *Your God Is Too Small*. In it, he insightfully argued that we have an unfortunate tendency to reduce the divine mystery to manageable but sadly mundane descriptions. We think of God as a cop, for example, or an angry parent, or a close buddy.

Comparisons such as these may be helpful at times. But if we take them too literally, Phillips warned, we distort God by squeezing him into utterly inadequate conceptual boxes. Our God becomes trivial and so does our spiritual life.

While I think Phillips is correct to caution us against our tendency to make God too small, I also suspect we're just as likely to fall into the opposite trap of making God too big.

Some of us, for example, think of God as an unapproachable potentate who dwells somewhere way out there in the cosmos. If we're extremely fortunate, one day we may be allowed into this celestial sultan's antechamber. But even then we'll be crushed with a sense of his utter grandeur and remoteness—something like the poor, cowering lion before the flaming, thundering Wizard of Oz.

Others of us conceive of God as a rather nebulous presence that permeates all reality without explicitly revealing himself in any particular aspect of it. It isn't that God is coy, but rather that the world in which we live simply can't contain his infinite and eternal nature. So even though God is always somehow present, this presence is only vague and, for the most part, inaccessible. God, then, is disconcertingly absent from the physical realm in which we live and breathe.

In both of these cases, our God is too big. The notion of God as potentate is connected with a rather immature understanding of majesty as imperious pomp and circumstance. The belief that God is too immense for our smallish world confuses infinity, which is a spiritual category, and space, a physical one.

The consequence of either of these ways of thinking is that we alienate ourselves from God because we've made him too big to relate to. Who can love a potentate? Who can adore or praise a hazy, ineluctable presence?

The heart of Christianity is the great and incomprehensible truth that God's true majesty, God's authentic immensity, consists in God's willingness to become lowly and forsaken, to pitch a tent among us and become one of us. God's presence is sometimes revealed in lightning and thunder and smoke on Mount Sinai, but it's much more likely to show up in the faces of our neighbors. And not just our respectable neighbors, either, but those whom we generally go out of our way to avoid: the poor, the ill, the imprisoned, the aged, the weak, and the despised.

In their faces, if we but have eyes to see, we encounter God. In their lowliness and helplessness we discover the real majesty of a God of love and self-sacrifice.

This is a bitter pill for those who prefer God well-scrubbed and polite. The youthful Francis certainly found it so. He was willing to serve God, but he preferred his Master to be respectably groomed. That's why God, who cares nothing for social status, nudged him toward a better understanding of divine majesty by appearing to him as a leper.

When Francis saw the leper coming, he shrank in disgust. Nothing could have possibly been more revolting than this wraith with filthy garments and oozing, caved-in face.

Yet, when Francis dismounted, walked over to the leper, and fearfully gazed into his face, he saw something there that he hadn't expected. He looked into those eyes filled with pain and loneliness and saw Christ staring back at him. Then he eagerly embraced and kissed the leper, realizing what he'd never known before: the Lord whom he was seeking to serve was *there*, in the suffering of the leper, as well as in the broken bodies and spirits of all who wander the earth with no place to lay their heads.

The moment this truth broke in on Francis, his God ceased being too big—and also too small, for that matter.

FOR REFLECTION

Is your God too big to reveal in the homeless, the broken, the suffering? If God isn't found in them, where is God found?

MEDITATION

God's temple is human history; the "sacred" transcends the narrow limits of the places of worship. We find the Lord in our encounters with others, especially the poor, marginalized, and exploited ones. An act of love towards them is an act of love toward God. This is why Yves Congar speaks of the "sacrament of our neighbor," who as a visible reality reveals to us and allows us to welcome the Lord.

—Gustavo Gutierrez, *Essential Writings*

CHAPTER SIX

~ What the Crucifix Said ~

FRANCIS'S WORDS

Francis quotes from John 8:47:

He who is of God hears the words of God.

—Letter to a General Chapter

MIRROR

Francis left the town one day to meditate out-of-doors and as he was passing by the church of San Damiano which was threatening to collapse with age, he felt urged to go in and pray. There as he knelt in prayer before a painted image of the Crucified, he felt greatly comforted in spirit and his eyes were full of tears as he gazed at the cross. Then, all of a sudden, he heard a voice coming from the cross and telling him three times, "Francis, go and repair my house. You see it is all falling down."

—Bonaventure, *Life of St. Francis*

FEW STORIES ABOUT FRANCIS ARE AS WELL-KNOWN AS HIS mystical summons by the San Damiano crucifix to "repair my church." The event most likely occurred in the fall of 1205 when Francis was twenty-four years old. He had abandoned his fantasies of martial glory to enlist in the service of God but hadn't yet quite figured out what God wanted him to do.

The mysterious voice from the Byzantine crucifix gave him a sense of direction. For the next two years Francis labored to rebuild the broken-down church of San Damiano, begging stones and mortar from the amused townspeople of Assisi.

"Good people!" he cried in the town square. "Give me stones! One stone gets you one blessing! Two get you two blessings! Three get you three blessings!" It was the beginning of his public ministry, and it seemed quite ludicrous to nearly everyone.

The standard interpretation of the San Damiano story is that God was really telling St. Francis to rebuild the corruption-riddled Church, not poor little San Damiano chapel. But my guess is that the summons included both. All of us must begin somewhere, and even the greatest missions have small beginnings. Lugging stones and propping up the walls of an aged and tottering chapel is a good apprenticeship for strengthening the spiritual foundations of Mother Church.

Focusing too closely on the standard interpretation of San Damiano risks blinding us to an important message in the story: God's will for us always surpasses our power of comprehension. God says, "Repair my house," and we, because of our limited vision and timid imagination, suppose that the most God wants from us is a little hammering here, a little wallpapering there.

What God really intends unfolds only with time, prayer, and discernment, and even then there remains a mysterious edge to it that's forever beyond our ken. What mortal can fathom the divine plan? This, at least, was Francis's experience.

There are three lessons here.

First, those of us who strain to hear God's voice ought not to be so eager to receive unambiguous instructions that we ignore any communication that isn't crystal clear. Given the disparity between our mortal receptors and the divine transmitter, such selectivity is foolish. Even worse, it's arrogant, constituting as it does a demand that God behave in ways that we think proper. We need to remember that God's voice is subtler than a black-and-white sheet of instructions from a technical manual. Otherwise, as J.B. Phillips has already warned us, we make God too little.

Second, remain open to the multitude of possibilities embedded in any divine communication. When God whispers in your ear, realize that you hear only the topmost layer of what God wishes to impress on you. Take time to mull the message over in order to explore its depths and to make sure that you really hear what God has to say, not what you think God ought to say. Sometimes your exploration will take you in totally unanticipated directions of service. How could Francis, kneeling before the altar in San Damiano, have possibly guessed what God had in store for him?

And third, think big when it comes to interpreting God's voice. Thinking big doesn't mean putting the most dramatic or earth-shaking spin on the summons, but rather appreciating the fact that whatever God is leading you to do is immeasurably important simply because it's God's wish. Had Francis's only job been to repair San Damiano, that task would have been the grandest thing in his life because it was the one given him by God.

So think big. Know that God speaks to you, and that when God does, your assigned task, whatever it is, regardless of how modest it appears in the eyes of the world, takes on eternal importance.

FOR REFLECTION

Do you demand crystal-clear marching orders from God before you're willing to act? If so, are you being scrupulous—or arrogant?

MEDITATION

The Holy Spirit writes no more Gospels except in our hearts. All we do from moment to moment is live this new Gospel of the Holy Spirit. We, if we are holy, are the paper; our sufferings and our actions are the ink. The workings of the Holy Spirit are his pen, and with it he writes a living Gospel....

Just think what an infinite number of different and worthwhile books are produced by the mixing up of twenty-six letters. We cannot understand this wonder, so how can we comprehend what God is doing in the universe? How can we read and understand so vast a book, one in which every single letter has its own special meaning and within its tiny shape, contains the most profound mysteries? We can neither see nor feel these mysteries. Only by faith can they be known.

—Jean-Pierre de Caussade, *Abandonment to Divine Providence*

CHAPTER SEVEN

~ Going Under ~

FRANCIS'S WORDS

Almighty, eternal, just and merciful God, grant us…that, cleansed
and enlightened interiorly and fired with the ardour of the Holy
Spirit, we may be able to follow in the footsteps of your Son, our
Lord Jesus Christ, and so make our way to you.

—Letter to a General Chapter

MIRROR

Francis was still a recent recruit to the service of Christ; and when
he heard of the threats of his pursuers, foreseeing their arrival, he
hid from his father's anger by creeping into a secret cave which he
had prepared as a refuge. There he stayed for a whole month; and
only one person in his father's house knew of his hiding place. He
ate the food brought to him secretly and prayed continually with
many tears that the Lord would deliver him from such persecu-
tion and grant him the fulfilment of his desire.

He prayed unceasingly with tears and fasting, not relying on
his own industry or virtue, but placing all his trust in God; and
although he was still in the darkness of the world the Lord filled
his soul with ineffable joy and a wonderful light.

—The Legend of the Three Companions

WHILE FRANCIS WAS HARD AT WORK REBUILDING SAN DAMIANO,
Pietro di Bernardone decided that enough was enough. If this

harebrained whelp of his wouldn't listen to reason, there was nothing left but to seize him and beat some sense into him. So Pietro gathered together his bondsmen and raced for San Damiano in search of his prodigal son.

When Francis heard that Pietro was coming, fear got the better of him and he squirreled away in a hiding place he'd discovered while working on San Damiano. In all likelihood it was a concealed pit (an *occulta fovea*, as the Latin text says) under the church's flooring, probably right next to the altar. Such secret places, dug to hide parish silver and gold from marauders, were common in churches of Francis's day. Francis remained there a whole month—the story's time frame is obviously meant to remind us of Jesus's forty days and nights in the wilderness— whimpering in the dark, too frightened to come out even to wash or eat, all the while tearfully begging God to turn his father's heart, or at least his heavy fist.

On the surface of things, this story doesn't show Francis in a particularly good light. This is the way a knight of Christ behaves? Surely it would have been nobler on his part to have faced up to his father. There's something shameful about cowering in a pit; it's the act of a coward.

But in a God-saturated universe, nothing's ever quite what it appears to be. Even the most commonplace events conceal a deep spiritual meaning. What seems an act of craven cowardice to the eyes of the world can actually be an act of incredible courage.

So it was in this case. For in crawling into San Damiano's hidden pit, Francis gave himself up to an ordeal much more agonizing than anything his father could have inflicted on him. Bernardone's rage was the occasion for Francis's retreat, but the meaning of his action went far beyond a family squabble.

If one examines legends and myths of heroes who go on spiritual quests—and Francis is surely such a person—one discovers several common themes. These themes appear in story after story of spiritual seeking, regardless of the culture or religion from which they spring. There's good reason for this: they're expressions of universal experiences.

One of these themes is the experience of going under. At some point in the spiritual journey, the hero in search of God must die, so to speak, and this death is usually symbolized by a descent into a grave of sorts. The hero may dive into the ocean's depths, or plunge into a dark valley, or crawl into an unexplored cave—or, as in Francis's case, hide away in an *occulta fovea*. Each of these possibilities is a symbolic utterance of a shared spiritual intuition that it's necessary for the God-seeker to die to his or her old self in order to find God. New life comes only if the husk withers.

In the Russian Orthodox tradition, the going-under place where spiritual heroes are slain to be reborn is called *poustinia*. The word literally means "desert," but it's come to signify the spiritual stripping down that occurs when we dive deeply into our soul, touch base with the indwelling Spirit that awaits us there, and realize that our usual me-centered existence has created a wall between ourselves and God.

When we go into the inner desert, we appreciate for the first time just how much unnecessary baggage we carry around. We see and gasp at the incredible artificiality of our old way of life, the flimsiness of our old values, the duplicity of our old self. The process is harrowing because it rips away everything by which we've defined ourselves. But this desert dying, this going under, is a necessary condition for the kind of "ineffable joy" and "wonderful light" that suffused Francis at the end of his time in the pit.

In fact, then, Francis's retreat to the *poustinia* brought to climax the first stage of his spiritual journey: the cumulative loss of his addiction to desperate revelry, his noble ambitions, his confused notions of God. His death in the darkness was the final purging his soul needed to stand upright before the master. The going under was brutal, for the *poustinia*—make no mistake about it—is the God-seeker's Calvary. But only from Calvary comes resurrection.

FOR REFLECTION

Poustinia, the place of stripping, death, and rebirth, is different for different people. For Francis, it was a pit at San Damiano. For Jonah, it was a whale. For Jesus, the Judean wilderness. If you've yet to go under, what do you think your *poustinia* will look like?

MEDITATION

It is not enough to lead a life of dedication and surrender as so many of the religious orders do. Every Christian must do more—with vows or without vows—wherever they are, whoever they may be!

That "more" can be a *poustinia*, an entry into the desert, a lonely place, a silent place, where one can lift the two arms of prayer and penance to God in atonement, intercession, reparation for one's sins and those of one's brothers. *Poustinia* is the place where we can go in order to gather courage to speak the words of truth, remembering that truth is God, and that we proclaim the word of God. The *poustinia* will cleanse us and prepare us to do so, like the burning coal the angel placed on the lips of the prophet.

—Catherine de Hueck Doherty, *Poustinia:*
Christian Spirituality of the East for Western Man

CHAPTER EIGHT

~ Naked ~

FRANCIS'S WORDS

Keep nothing for yourselves, so that He who has given himself wholly to you may receive you wholly.

—Letter to a General Chapter

MIRROR

Francis's father Pietro arranged to have Francis brought before the bishop of the diocese, where he should renounce all his claims and return everything he had. In his genuine love for poverty, Francis was more than ready to comply and he willingly appeared before the bishop. There he made no delay—without hestitation, without hearing or saying a word—he immediately took off his clothes and gave them back to his father. Then it was discovered that he wore a hair-shirt under his fine clothes next to his skin. He even took off his trousers in his fervor and enthusiasm and stood there naked before them all. Then he said to his father, "Until now I called you my father, but from now on I can say without reserve, 'Our Father who art in heaven.' He is all my wealth and I place all my confidence in him."

—Bonaventure, Life of St. Francis

THE UNFORGETTABLE STORY OF FRANCIS'S NAKEDNESS IN THE town square of Assisi has been told hundreds of times, both before and since it was chronicled by Bonaventure, a theologian and early biographer of the saint (and himself a saint!) But the tale never loses its wonderment.

Pietro di Bernardone has at last captured his lunatic son. In a rage, he drags the youth, still filthy from his thirty days in the hiding place, before Guido, Assisi's bishop and spiritual leader. "This ungrateful boy has shamed me with his ridiculous behavior!" Pietro cries. "He disrespects his own father! Tell him to straighten up, your Grace! He'll obey you!"

The gleeful townspeople have gathered to watch the show. It's not every day such free entertainment comes their way.

Then Francis exceeds the crowd's wildest expectations. Instead of either defending himself or asking pardon, he there and then strips off the remaining pieces of clothing given him by his father, returns them to Pietro, and announces that from now on his only father is God. The crowd gasps in amazement, Pietro (who for all his bluster still loves his son) cringes at the awful finality of Francis's words, and Bishop Guido, not quite knowing what else to do, covers Francis's nakedness with his cloak.

There are few moments in the history of Christianity more gripping. This is the kind of high drama from which legends are born.

What sense can we make of this event? Pious authors such as Bonaventure like to see it as symbolic of Francis's renunciation of the world and his newly chosen loyalty to the Church. I don't necessarily disagree with this interpretation. But I think we can excavate a deeper layer of meaning from the story, one hinted at in our own time by Franco Zeffirelli's film *Brother Sun, Sister Moon*.

In the movie, Zeffirelli starts out by following the traditional story line: Pietro rages before the bishop, furiously shouting that he's given Francis everything he ever wanted. But the zinger comes when it's Francis's turn to speak. Responding to his father's anger and Guido's bewilderment, Francis exultantly says this:

I want to be happy! I want to live like the birds in the sky. I want to experience the purity and freedom that they experience. The rest is of no use to me. If the purpose of life is this loveless toil we fill our days with, then it's not for me. There has to be something better. Man is a spirit! He has a soul! And that—that is what I want to recapture!

With these words, Francis proclaims the two goals he'll pursue for the rest of his life: freedom and joy. Ever since his madcap youth, he'd been searching for them. In his innocence, he'd fancied they were to be found in wine and song or military glory.

Now he knows better. The vision in front of San Damiano's crucifix, his unexpected encounter with the mysterious leper, and most recently, his spiritual battle in the *poustinia* have convinced him otherwise. True freedom and joy aren't dependent on the things of the world. They're interior states—or, better, interior gifts—bestowed on yearning hearts by a gracious God.

Francis will learn more and more about the meaning of freedom and joy as his spiritual journey continues. But what he's discovered thus far, and what he tries to express by stripping himself naked in Assisi's square, is that the first step in attaining freedom is getting free of oneself, and that freedom from oneself in turn is a necessary condition for perfect joy. Francis had been shedding himself during the months preceding the dramatic event in the town square—shedding his old ambitions, self-centeredness, vanity. In doing so, he placed himself utterly in the hands of God: From now on, he declares, God is my only Father!

This realization, of course, calls for an act of loving trust whose audacity takes the breath away. How many of us would dare to burn our bridges so completely? But there was a passion moving Francis more compelling than the human urge to play it safe.

He wanted to know God as God is, not as the world imagines God to be. He wanted to open his heart to the living God, to experience God with the palpable immediacy with which you and I experience sunlight or flame. And to do this, Francis realized that he had to get out of the way so that God could come to him, unfiltered, pure, unadorned. Francis's nakedness was an invitation to God.

Francis's act of public nakedness is also symbolic of the single-mindedness with which he will seek God for the rest of his days. The anonymous author of a medieval spiritual classic entitled *The Cloud of Unknowing* says that Christians ought to cultivate a "naked intent" toward God. The use of the word *naked* is significant. At the very least, it suggests that our yearning for God should be transparently pure rather than surreptitiously clothed in mere theological curiosity or the desire for social respectability. God should be the sole target at which we aim, and we should aim at

God solely for God's sake, regardless of the cost. To nakedly intend toward God, we must stand naked before God.

Francis gave up more than a bundle of clothing on that fateful day in the Assisi square. He handed over his old self as well. Francis tied up the old Francis, tossed him aside, and stepped out into the sunlight, naked as the day he was born, ready to begin anew.

FOR REFLECTION

Does the prospect of utter nakedness before God and your fellow humans frighten or even terrify you? Or does its promise of immediate contact with God excite you?

MEDITATION

It was naked faith that attracted me. This alone seemed the anchor of salvation for my weary spirit.

Any cultural cloak for the Word seemed a distortion.

Any attempt at compromise seemed an enfeeblement of my urge to follow Christ Crucified....

No longer did I seek miraculous or mystical signs of his activity. I sought the nakedness of his presence.

No longer did I wish to discuss him. I wanted to know him.

No longer did I seek the rapport with him I had so often enjoyed in the Sunday liturgy—which can so easily give you the illusion of being "right where it's at," with its rites and ceremonies. Now I desired his intimacy in the nakedness of matter, in the transparency of light, in the toil of loving my fellow human beings.

—Carlo Caretto, *I Sought and I Found*

CHAPTER NINE

~ Vocation ~

FRANCIS'S WORDS

In whatever way you think you will best please our Lord God and follow in his footsteps and in poverty, take that way with the Lord God's blessing.

—A Letter to Brother Leo

MIRROR

One day during the celebration of Mass he heard the words in which Christ bade his disciples go out and preach, carrying neither gold nor silver, nor haversack for the journey, without staff, bread, or shoes, and having no second garment. After listening to the priest's explanation of these words of the Gospel, full of unspeakable joy, he exclaimed: "This is what my whole heart desires to accomplish."

—The Legend of the Three Companions

GETTING NAKED BEFORE GOD IS A GIGANTIC STEP IN THE RIGHT direction, but it's not enough. As Christians, we're called not just to open ourselves to God, but to place ourselves in God's service. This obviously means that all of us need to discover how we can best serve God. Each of us is a unique personality with specific strengths and weaknesses. How are we being called to transform our strengths—and, just as importantly, our weaknesses—into actions pleasing to the Creator?

The nature of vocation in Christian life is memorably expressed in Matthew's Gospel when Jesus invites his followers to bear his "yoke" (see Matthew 11:29–30). In the ancient Near East, a yoke was carved to fit the contours of the individual ox's back upon which it would rest. The wise husbandman knew that one size didn't fit all, that each animal possessed strengths and weaknesses all its own.

In using the image of the yoke, Jesus is implying that vocations are likewise tailor-made to fit their bearers. That's one of the reasons why they're "light" and "easy": The vocational burden laid on our shoulders is precisely the one we're best equipped to carry.

Francis discovered his own unique calling—his own *vocation*, from the Latin *vocare*, "to call"—sometime after he publicly resolved in Assisi's square to open himself fully to God. The Gospel spoke to him one day at Mass. He heard, as if for the first time, Jesus's instructions to the apostles to adopt a life of voluntary poverty, tying themselves to no possessions so that they might be totally free to serve God and spread the Good News.

The moment Francis heard these words, his heart told him this was the path God was calling him to follow. He was filled with "unspeakable joy," as *The Legend of the Three Companions* tells us, and this joy was but a foretaste of the ecstasies in store for him.

Some Christians discover their vocations at the very beginning of their faith journey. For others, the realization of what they've been called to do comes more slowly. There may be several misdirections before awareness of God's intentions sinks in. But whether it comes early or late, a sense of vocation is essential. Without it, faith runs the risk of being purely cerebral, a no-risk and rather comfortable acquiescence to a lifeless set of beliefs.

Christianity isn't an abstract philosophy. It's a complete way of life. Consequently, profession of belief in Christianity isn't simply an intellectual nod of the head, but a commitment to live in such a way as to express concretely one's convictions in the everyday world. Such engagement demands a sense of direction, a sense of individual mission and purpose. This is supplied by the particular vocation each of us is given. When we discover our own unique calling, regardless of what it may be, we find the spiritual true north by which to plot our course.

Two points need to be remembered when it comes to vocation. The first is that vocation isn't a choice on our part. We don't select our vocation from a number of available possibilities. It's not a question of which career we'll pursue or what style of shoes we'll buy. A vocation is designed for us by God. Our job is to recognize what it is through a process of prayerful discernment. We may then, of course, choose to accept or reject it.

The second point is that the discovery of our true vocation brings us great joy and excitement because it holds before us the promise of fulfillment and completion. This doesn't mean that a vocation will always be fun or pleasant. Doing what God calls us to do can be quite harrowing at times, demanding unforeseen sacrifices from us.

Our vocation can take us in directions we do not wish to go, at least initially. Despite that, it's an occasion for joy, because once we discover our vocation, we grow in awareness of who we are and why we were made. If we refuse to accept our God-given vocations, out of either fear or sheer mule-headedness, we just might be able to coast through life with little or no pain or hardship (although I personally doubt it). But we do so at the cost of never becoming who we can and should be.

For Reflection

Have you discovered a vocation yet? Does it bring you a joyful sense of fulfillment, even though it may be hard at times? If not, perhaps it's not your true vocation, and you ought to open yourself to new possibilities.

Meditation

Vocation is God's call to undertake such-and-such a sort of holy life in preference to all others, his urgent call to each individual soul to sanctify itself in this particular way. There can never be any question of choosing a vocation: the word "choice" is excluded by the word "vocation," which means "calling," a call from God. Therefore we do not "choose a vocation" but seek to find our vocation, to do all we can to hear the divine Voice calling us, to make sure what he is saying—and then to obey him. Where vocation is concerned, God speaks, calls, commands: man has not to choose but to listen and obey.

—Charles de Foucauld, *Writings*

CHAPTER TEN

~ *Theia Mania* ~

FRANCIS'S WORDS

The Lord told me what He wanted: He wanted me to be a new fool in the world.

—*The Assisi Compilation*

MIRROR

"Hear, Brothers," Francis sang, "hear the new madness!"

Everyone was roaring with laughter. The young men began to whistle, meow, and bark to drown out his voice....

Francis mounted the steps of the temple, opened his arms to the jeering crowd, and screamed: "Love! Love! Love!"

—Nikos Kazantzakis, *Saint Francis*

FROM THE VERY BEGINNING OF HIS PUBLIC MINISTRY, FRANCIS WAS accused of being insane. How else to explain the behavior of a young man who threw away wealth and privilege to dress in filthy rags, kiss lepers, putter around fallen-down churches, and beg in the streets? Sometimes the people laughingly jeered at him; at other times, they were less gentle, shoving and even striking him out of sheer exasperation with his strange ways. Almost everyone wrote him off as a madman.

We should all be so mad. Madness in the service of God is holy.

At the beginning of the Christian era, St. Paul quickly recognized that true followers of Christ would act in such a way as to appear bonkers to everyone else. Their behavior would seem absolutely foolish in the eyes of the sophisticated and worldly (see 1 Corinthians 1:18–25).

Why is this so? What exactly is it about Christianity that strikes the world as crazy? Some critics will say that it's the bizarre set of beliefs accepted by Christians: God is three but also one, Jesus Christ is both fully human and fully God, and so on. Surely no right-thinking person could believe such gibberish!

Others will insist that the Christian's willingness to pay allegiance to an unseen spiritual world is mad when there's so much worldly pleasure to be derived from this one. Why deprive yourself for the sake of pie in the sky?

Still others will assert that the values by which Christians try to live—mercy, meekness, compassion, sacrifice—are self-handicapping to the point of foolishness. It's hard enough to get ahead in the world. Why make things tougher on yourself?

But when you look beneath the surface of these criticisms, you discover that what the world really finds offensive, what it sees as truly insane, is Christianity's unapologetic celebration of love. A world too cynical or selfish or indifferent to love unreservedly is bound to be so baffled by people who do that it dismisses them as crazy—and sometimes dangerously so. This is the great insight behind novelist Nikos Kazantzakis's fictional portrait of St. Francis.

And why is Christian love mocked as a kind of madness? Because the profligate lover—the lover who, like Francis, draws no boundaries around love, who lovingly embraces all of creation—no longer sees himself or herself as the center of the universe. Egoism and selfishness are swept away by love's rush to serve the beloved.

Love focuses on the beloved to the exclusion of the lover's own desires or interests. The person consumed by love doesn't hesitate for one instant to place himself or herself in the service of the beloved, even if doing so seems foolish. This self-sacrifice on the lover's part is madness to a culture that places self-interest above every other motive.

Loving in this way makes the lover radically vulnerable—remember Francis's nakedness in Assisi's town square?—and this is undoubtedly another reason that the world sees it as insane. To love as Francis did is to be willing to make oneself utterly available for others, to give to them unstintingly just as God in Christ gives himself to humanity.

Unscrupulous persons will take advantage of that love, manipulating it for their gain. Hostile or suspicious persons will coldly rebuff the love offered them. The needy and weak will smother the lover who extends a helping hand. There is a cost attached to profligate love. It bankrupts the person who flings it about. But it also enriches him or her in unimaginable ways.

Truth be told, the person possessed by love is mad, as the ancient Greeks recognized, because he's under the control of a force greater than his own will. Even today, our ordinary language reflects this old way of thinking; we say that "she's crazy with love" or "he's out of his head with love."

According to the philosopher Plato, a person who genuinely loves is possessed by a divine spirit who acts in and through his or her body and mind and will. The lover, in other words, is so filled with God—so immeasurably enriched by God—that his way of loving takes on a Godlike, no-holds-barred generosity. Thus the Greeks frequently referred to love as *theia mania*, the "divine madness." For the Christian, this should become a familiar idea. When we love—really, *really* love—the God who is Love enters us and by grace fills us with his Spirit.

What could be crazier? What could be better?

For Reflection

Have you ever felt frenzied with love for God and God's creation? Or do you refuse to allow yourself to let go because you fear the loss of self-control?

Meditation

Because [the lover] stands apart from the common objects of human ambition and applies himself to the divine, he is reproached by most men for being out of his wits; they do not realize that he is in fact possessed by a god.

—Plato, *Phaedrus*

CHAPTER ELEVEN

~ Lady Poverty ~

FRANCIS'S WORDS

Holy Poverty puts to shame
all greed, avarice,
and all the anxieties of this life

—*The Praises of the Virtues*

MIRROR

The brothers often asked the advice of the Bishop, who received
Francis with kindness, but said: "It seems to me that it is very
hard and difficult to possess nothing in the world." To this blessed
Francis replied: "My Lord, if we had any possessions we should
also be forced to have arms to protect them, since possessions are
a cause of disputes and strife, and in many ways we should be
hindered from loving God and our neighbor. Therefore in this life
we wish to have no temporal possessions."

—*The Legend of the Three Companions*

WHENEVER ANYONE THINKS OF FRANCIS, VOLUNTARY POVERTY
instantly comes to mind. For centuries now he's been affectionately
called *il Poverello*, the "little poor man." We've already seen how
he renounced his worldly inheritance in Assisi's town square, and
how he discovered his vocation after hearing the Gospel account of
how Christ urged his followers to live in poverty.

In the Rule he eventually wrote for the companions who came to live in community with him at la Portiuncula, Francis expressly warns against the perils of ownership. As for himself, he was perfectly indifferent to possessions, more than willing to give away his cloak or meal to anyone in need. All that mattered to him was fidelity to what he lovingly called "Lady Poverty," the damsel to whom he, a knight of Christ, had pledged himself.

Francis's unapologetic espousal of radical poverty, which he saw as a way of honoring and imitating Jesus, the poor man who had no place to lay his head, inevitably strikes people in a number of ways. Some—although a very few—are so intensely attracted to his renunciatory way of life that they adopt it as their own. Others abstractly admire his desire to be free of ownership, but reluctantly conclude that Francis took the ideal of poverty too far. Still others are outright repulsed by what they see as his pathological extremism. Surely, they insist, God can't wish us to be filthy, homeless beggars.

Each of us must decide how to respond to the Lady Poverty so cherished by Francis. But regardless of where we fall on the spectrum, few of us will feel up to quibbling with the spirit behind Franciscan poverty. At the very least, Lady Poverty warns us against the chronic temptation of consumerism that besets our society today.

Examine your own life and your own conscience. How much of what you own is necessary, and how much of it is just stuff that somehow has piled up over the years? Do you really need two or three vehicles, a smartphone, a tablet, and a laptop, or thousands of dollars' worth of sound equipment? Do you need to move into a larger house every seven or so years, or vacation at increasingly exotic spots?

There comes a point where the possessions with which we surround ourselves not only cease to offer us pleasure but actually become burdensome. We worry about losing them through theft or fire or economic downswing. We enviously compare them with the better possessions owned by neighbors or relatives. We nearly kill ourselves working longer hours to make more money...to buy more stuff.

Where does it all end? Is this how humans should live? Is this the way to freedom and joy?

One of the more pernicious consequences of the spirit of consumerism is that it tends to influence the way we view each other. Other people begin to take on the status of exchangeable and usable commodities in our eyes, as things to be manipulated for our benefit, or as Francis suggested in his reply to Bishop Guido, they're seen as competitors (and hence enemies) for the material goodies we crave. Either way, their essential Godlikeness is ignored, and the outcome is that we do damage to them, to our own spiritual health, and to God's creation.

There's another essential point that Francis's espousal of Lady Poverty should bring to mind: The more we accumulate, the less there is for others who live in genuine need. A popular bumper sticker advises us to "live simply so that others may simply live."

This isn't just a clever wordplay. As a nation, the United States uses (and frequently wastes) inordinate percentages of the world's fuel supplies and foodstuffs.

As individuals, many of us insist on owning more than we actually need to live comfortably, while turning a blind eye to those unfortunates in our communities who barely scrape together a living. Voluntary poverty is a spiritual choice that can bestow freedom upon its practitioners, but economic penury always enslaves and brutalizes its victims. Both Francis and Jesus before him recognized the difference between the two and adopted the one in part as a strategy for redressing the other. How can we who claim to walk the Christian path do any less?

FOR REFLECTION

Take stock of your lifestyle. Do you feel weighed down and possibly even enslaved by all the things you own? In what ways can you live more simply so that others may simply live?

MEDITATION

Poverty was the virtue that was to impart originality to the Franciscan Order and constitute its "true foundation."

Voluntarily poor one may be from philosophy or asceticism, for reasons of zeal, of charity, and others still. But Francis was poor from love.

In truth it was a marvelous union. Never was a loved woman the object of a more chivalrous and loyal cult, of more impassioned and charming homage.

—Omer Englebert, *St. Francis of Assisi*

CHAPTER TWELVE

~ Holy Simplicity ~

FRANCIS'S WORDS

Those brothers of mine who are led by curiosity for knowledge will find themselves empty-handed on the day of reckoning.

—*The Assisi Compilation*

MIRROR

When a certain minister asked that some magnificent and very valuable books be kept with Francis's permission, he heard this from him: "I do not want to lose the book of the Gospel, which we have been promised, for your books. You may do as you please, but my permission will not be made a trap."

—Thomas of Celano, *Second Life of Francis*

AN EMBRACE OF LADY POVERTY MEANS THAT WE TRY TO LIVE freely by getting out from under the possessions that own us. This can range from adopting a Franciscan-like life of voluntary poverty to the more common effort to cut down on consumption of needless luxuries. The purpose in either case is to forgo what we don't need in order to imitate better the holy poverty of Christ, to appreciate better our fellow humans, and to contribute to a more equitable distribution of resources.

But genuine freedom—which, recall, is a necessary condition for the joy Francis craves—isn't simply a matter of throwing off externalities that burden us. It entails a relinquishment of internal acquisitiveness. In addition to ridding ourselves of goods that weigh down our spirits, we must wean ourselves from our psychological desire for them. Doing the one without the other simply won't suffice. We can steel ourselves to a life of material poverty yet still remain enslaved by our lusts, vanity, and jealousies.

"Holy Simplicity" is the phrase Francis typically used to describe the internal state in which the will and mind have rediscovered the childlike innocence with which they were originally endowed by God. Jesus taught that Christians must once again become like little children—another kind of madness in the eyes of the world!—and this means minimally that we find a way to tame the hornet's nest of buzzing ambitions and stinging drives that beset most supposedly mature adults.

Besides old-fashioned greed, one of the ways we commonly sin against Holy Simplicity is by overintellectualizing our faith. Early on in the Order, a conflict arose between those who thought that a holy life was one of simple trust and obedience and those who believed that it also included intellectual ownership of theology and philosophy. Francis pulled no punches in his conviction that "book learning" violated the spirit of simplicity. He feared that study of theology could become an end in itself, diverting students and scholars from a living commitment to the spirit of the Gospel for the sake of an overly cerebral analysis of its letter.

Such an approach runs the risk of breeding intellectual arrogance along with an accompanying sense of possessiveness that values one's own pet interpretation of Scripture over anyone else's. Even worse, it can mutate into an activity motivated not by the desire to glorify God, but by the desire to make a name for oneself as a learned pundit. If either of these possibilities emerge, the scholar has allowed himself or herself to become enslaved by ambitions and drives and addictions and jealousies. Holy Simplicity is lost.

Because he believed that such scholarship was a threat to Holy Simplicity, Francis has frequently been accused of advocating an irrational anti-intellectualism. But I think this overstates the case. Far better, I believe, to read his remarks as an illustration of what can happen when we abandon simplicity by vainly presuming that the better read in theology or scriptural exegesis we are, the holier we become.

Using the mind to serve God is a legitimate path for some Christians; as we've already seen, vocations differ from person to person. But surely there comes a point where we can become so invested in our own clever ideas about God that we focus on them instead of on God himself. Ideas are, after all, only interpretations of reality, and if we lose sight of this we can shut ourselves off from the very reality we hope to understand better through our theorizing.

So in reflecting on Francis's words about Holy Simplicity, ask yourself this question: At the end of the day, which is more valuable: knowing a lot about what people have written about God, or knowing God in a vital, everyday way? The two aren't always in conflict. But Francis is correct when he worries that the former can interfere with a naked intent toward one's Creator.

FOR REFLECTION

Do you find yourself reading book after book on prayer, but rarely praying? Devouring volumes on theology, but rarely opening the Bible? Scrutinizing canon law, but turning a blind eye to your own behavior?

MEDITATION

A certain philosopher asked St. Anthony: "Father, how can you be so happy when you are deprived of books?" Anthony replied: "My book, O philosopher, is the nature of created things, and any time I want to read the words of God, the book is before me."

—Thomas Merton, *Wisdom of the Desert*

CHAPTER THIRTEEN

~ Gracious Humility ~

FRANCIS'S WORDS

No one should flatter himself with evil praise over what a sinner can do. A sinner can fast, pray, weep, mortify his flesh. This, however, he cannot do, namely, be faithful to his Lord. Therefore in this should we glory, that we give glory to God, that we serve him faithfully, that we ascribe to him whatever he has given us.

—Thomas of Celano, *Second Life of Francis*

MIRROR

When one day he was riding on an ass, because weak and infirm as he was he could not go by foot, he passed through the field of a peasant who happened to be working there just then; the peasant ran over to him and asked solicitously if he were Brother Francis. When the man of God humbly replied that he was the man he was asking about, the peasant said: "Try to be as good as you are said to be by all men, for many put their trust in you. Therefore I admonish you never to be other than you are expected to be." But when the man of God Francis heard this, he got down from the ass and threw himself before the peasant and humbly kissed his feet, thanking him for being kind enough to give him this admonition.

—Thomas of Celano, *Second Life of Francis*

This is one of my favorite stories about Francis. I shake my head in amazement every time I read it. Here's Francis, one of the holiest men of his day, patiently listening to the finger-wagging admonition of a peasant who's obviously been disappointed by earlier charismatic leaders who failed to live up to their own PR. *The eyes of the whole world are on you!* the peasant scolds. *Don't let us down!* And Francis heeds the peasant with the same respect and attention he'd give the pope himself. There's no patronizing eye-rolling on his part, no angry word of dismissal, no impatient tug on the donkey's reins. Francis humbly listens, embraces, and thanks.

The humility exemplified by Francis here and everywhere is a natural companion to Lady Poverty and Holy Simplicity. Whoever renounces material possessions no longer feels the need to draw class distinctions based on social prestige, wealth, or power. Similarly, a person who has tamed the will's craving for acclaim and the mind's tendency to pigeonhole others into neat but contrived categories isn't likely to climb on a high horse when chastised by a simple peasant.

Those fortunate individuals who have achieved the freedom of poverty and the peace of simplicity are secure enough with who and what they are to heed counsel, whoever may give it. They are gracious enough to be humble.

Francis valued Gracious Humility for the same reason he so loved poverty and simplicity: It was a virtue preached and practiced by Jesus. The twentieth-century spiritual writer Henri Nouwen describes Jesus's humility as the path of "downward mobility." Society teaches us to strive for upward mobility—to climb as high up the ladder of success as we possibly can. In the process, of course, we typically become egomaniacs, hell-bent on advancing our own interests regardless of who gets in the way.

Nouwen tells us that downward mobility is the better course. In moving downward, we make less of ourselves so that we may make more of others. In moving downward, we open ourselves to the beauty and wisdom of others because we're not fixated on, and hence blinded by, ourselves. In moving downward, we invite others—and, indeed, all of creation—to be themselves, rather than what we want them to be in order to serve our interests.

The path of downward mobility is never an easy one. It goes counter to all our socialization. People who choose downward mobility can expect to be jeered at by their contemporaries. Their relatives are likely to scold them for wasting their talents, their acquaintances apt to write them off as losers. But the blessing of this path lies in that it allows a person to discover who he or she really is, to find the core that lies beneath all the layers of superimposed false selves.

It's no accident that the word *humility* is derived from the Latin word for "earth." Whoever practices humility discovers his or her true roots and returns to basics. Humans aren't made to be pushy, self-regarding, upwardly mobile climbers. This simply isn't our true nature.

We're made in the image of a loving, self-giving, compassionate God. When we practice humility, we reclaim our lineage. And in doing so, we reaffirm that humility is a gift from God, graciously bestowed on us so that we might grow into who we should be.

Perhaps the greatest insight that comes from true humility is the realization that we are nothing without God's sustaining presence and protection. Even our humble awareness of our own radical dependence is grace-given. So who are we to curtly dismiss advice from a peasant, much less to force others to do our bidding?

Francis frequently encouraged his brothers in humility by reminding them that humility isn't simply a virtue pleasing to God, but one practiced by God. God himself walks the path of downward mobility every time the Eucharist is celebrated. Each day, Francis said, the Master of the entire cosmos, the Creator of all that has been, is, and will be, humbles himself for our sake. Each day God graciously allows himself to take on the earthy forms of bread and wine so that the souls of people might be nourished and their hearts gladdened. With this daily example of self-humbling before our eyes, how could we not desire to join God on the path of Gracious Humility?

For Reflection

Which path do you travel: the one of upward mobility toward worldly success, or the one of downward mobility toward God—and your true self?

MEDITATION

Saint Francis always mentioned humility in the same breath with poverty. In a sense, they are the same—personal "without-ness." This is a fact, because all that we have is from God. This is an ideal, because we want to be without everything but God.

—Leonard Foley, *To Live as Francis Lived*

CHAPTER FOURTEEN

~ Be Not Afraid! ~

FRANCIS'S WORDS

Too much confidence makes one guard too little against the enemy. If the devil can get but one hair from a man, he will soon make it grow into a beam.

—Thomas of Celano, *Second Life of Francis*

MIRROR

One is tempted to view la Portiuncula as a kind of paradise, an uncomfortable paradise, to be sure, but a paradise nonetheless, because the comfort that we cling to with horrible cowardice becomes quite ridiculous when measured against the inner joy that the brothers lived on. Amidst the prayer, mortification, and poverty reigning there was a merriment such as few brotherhoods have known on earth. Freed from all their material goods, which they had discarded as so much ordure (*tanquam stercora*), they cast themselves upon God.

—Julien Green, *God's Fool*

OUR REFLECTIONS ON LADY POVERTY, HOLY SIMPLICITY, AND Gracious Humility have brought us ever closer to the secret of perfect joy. When Francis stripped naked in Assisi's square, we saw that the joy he sought was linked to freedom. The novelist Julien Green likewise saw that the connection between the two is unseverable. He tells us that the life Francis and his brothers lived at their makeshift monastery of la Portiuncula was joyful precisely because poverty, simplicity, and humility had liberated them.

What's still not entirely clear, however, is why the three virtues practiced and taught by Francis bring joy—much less merriment (as Green claims). It's pretty obvious that poverty, simplicity, and humility free us from our attachments to the things of the world. But why should this detachment in turn cause joy? Contentment, perhaps. But joy? Somehow, it seems too strong a word to use.

We can begin to get a handle on why spiritual freedom brings joy by considering this: the freedom that Francis sought—the same that Jesus Christ preached—defeats the oldest and deadliest foe humankind faces: fear. Spiritual freedom, which Lady Poverty, Holy Simplicity, and Gracious Humility prepare the way for, is essentially *freedom from fear*. This is the wonderful breakthrough Francis and his brothers at la Portiuncula make. They become victorious over fear, that horrible slayer of the human spirit.

They no longer fear losing material goods. Why? Because they have none! They no longer fear their own desires and lusts. Why? Because they've let them go. They no longer fear what a cynical or hostile world says of them or might do to them. Why? Because they know that their very being is in God's hands, and God is untouchable! They are liberated from fear's death grip.

How could they not be joyful, and even merry?

Dorothy Day has something interesting to say about freedom from fear. She claims that the ultimate source of our fear is our insistence on permanence in life—on what we typically call "security." We cling to possessions, social status, intellectual models, even to other people, because we fear change and want stability. We deceive ourselves into believing that we can force the world to cease spinning, thereby guaranteeing that our future will remain unthreateningly like our present. Most of all we fear illness and death, because with them comes the greatest insecurity of all.

But our timid desire to hold back the tide is absurd. Everything changes in this life; nothing remains the same for long. This means that the human condition is necessarily defined by a sense of precariousness, or what Day calls "precarity."

Unless we wish to cower in fear our entire life, we must learn to cease our physical and emotional clinging and accept and even embrace precarity. We can find the strength to do this only if we learn to trust that, whatever happens, we're in God's reliable hands. The moment that we begin to trust, precarity no longer strikes us as a fearful rip in the fabric of existence.

Instead, we see it as a wondrous source of novelty and opportunity. We accept ourselves for what we are: precarious creatures balancing on a tightrope between temporality and eternity. We accept existence for what it is: an unstoppable flow of frequently unpredictable experiences and events. And we exult because we know that, in a God-filled universe, precariousness is something to be celebrated rather than deplored.

What wonderful blessings poverty, simplicity, and humility give— the freedom from fear, the courage to trust, the joy to celebrate. No wonder the seemingly drab and broken-down Portiuncula seemed a paradise!

For Reflection

What would you give to be free of fear? Are you willing to forsake security for the sake of joy?

Meditation

"Be not afraid!" Christ addressed this invitation many times to those He met.... "Be not afraid!" These are not words said into a void. They are profoundly rooted in the Gospel. They are simply the words of Christ Himself. Of what should we not be afraid? We should not fear the truth about ourselves.

—John Paul II, *Crossing the Threshold of Hope*

CHAPTER FIFTEEN

~ Burning Love ~

FRANCIS'S WORDS

Holy Love puts to shame all the temptations
of the devil and the flesh
and all natural fear.

—The Praises of the Virtues

MIRROR

Francis burned for Christ, his Spouse; he seemed to be completely absorbed by the fire of divine love like a glowing coal.

Inflamed with that perfect love which drives out fear, he longed to offer himself as a living victim to God by the sword of martyrdom; in this way he could repay Christ for his love.

—Bonaventure, *Life of St. Francis*

WE TOOK A QUICK LOOK AT LOVE WHEN WE REFLECTED ON WHAT it means to be a fool for God. We saw then that genuine love is a madness of sorts because the lover is beside himself or herself, possessed by the spirit of the supreme Lover. Now it's time to consider that statement in light of what we discovered about precarity in the previous chapter.

The twelfth-century Cistercian Isaac of Stella wrote that God created us in order that we might be. At first glance, this seems so obvious that it isn't worth stating. But if we think about Isaac's claim a bit, a deeper meaning unfolds.

To be in the fullest sense of the expression is to exist in as complete a way as possible, to fulfill all the inherent possibilities with which one is endowed—to live up, in other words, to one's destiny. Failure to do so is to fall short of full being, and to live a life that, to one degree or another, is stunted.

The obvious question then is: What is human destiny? Christianity's answer is startling in both its promise of fulfillment and its burden of responsibility. The destiny of each human is to become Godlike. Be perfect, said Jesus, as your Father in heaven is perfect. We are made in the image of God—a human is by nature *imago Dei*, as the medievals used to say—and the closer we come to accepting and cooperating consciously with that nature, the closer we approach full being.

God is pure, unadulterated Love. Consequently, Godlikeness is measured in terms of love. The equation is beautifully simple: The more we love, the more Godlike we become until, like Francis, we are coals glowing in the eternal flame of Love itself.

Love, then, isn't just the feel-good emotion or mushy sentimentalism of popular culture. Love is an affirmation of being, a grand yea-saying to God, an exuberantly grateful celebration of creation, an awed acknowledgment that God's plan is wondrous.

Conversely, the opposite of love is more than just the absence of emotions we typically associate with it. Failure to love is nothing less than a negation of being, a dismal nay-saying to God, a deadly rejection of creation, a sinful slighting of God's plan. The absence of love pulls us away from full being and hurls us into a state of relative nothingness. St. Paul recognized as much when he claimed that the wages of sin is death, void, vacuum—radical separation from the source of life and love (see Romans 6:23). Hell, as Dostoevsky once wrote, is not to love.

St. John noted something else about love: fear and love are incompatible (see 1 John 4:18). Ordinary experience attests to the truth of this claim, doesn't it? How many marriages have collapsed because of the fearful jealousy of one of the partners? How many friendships have shattered for similar reasons? Where there is fear, there is no room for genuine affirmation, genuine celebration, or the intensely profligate yea-saying of love.

It follows from this that freedom from fear, the blessing bestowed on us when we practice poverty, simplicity, and humility, liberates us to love. "Perfect love casts out fear," remarks St. John (1 John 4:18). But it's also the case that perfect freedom from fear allows opportunity for love. An affirmation of God's plan and our role in it can only be given when we find the courage to trust God despite the obvious precarity of human existence.

Genuine love, the love that consumes us in a never-quenched flame, is indeed a kind of foolishness. It takes us out of our fearful, egoistic, partial existences and throws us into the furnace of divine Love, which is also our own final and true identity. When we reach this height we're finally capable of the perfect joy Francis sought and found.

For Reflection

Is your way of living a resounding *Yes!* or a timid *Maybe?*

MEDITATION

In truth, each of us is called to respond to a universal note with a pure and unutterable harmony. As God's love progresses in our hearts, we will sense the exuberant simplicity of a thrust where the nuance of passion and action will combine themselves, and we will come closer to the full expression of our personality.

—Pierre Teilhard de Chardin, *The Spiritual Phenomenon*

CHAPTER SIXTEEN

~ The Joy Test ~

FRANCIS'S WORDS

There is one thing of which we can boast; we can boast of our humiliations and in taking up daily the holy cross of our Lord Jesus Christ.

—Admonitions

MIRROR

Francis called Brother Leo and said: "Brother Leo, write this down."

He answered: "I'm ready."

"Write what true joy is," Francis said. "A messenger comes and says that all the masters of theology in Paris have joined the Order—write: that is not true joy. Or all the prelates beyond the mountains—archbishops and bishops, or the King of France and the King of England—write: that is not true joy. Or that my friars have gone to the unbelievers and have converted all of them to the faith; or that I have so much grace from God that I heal the sick and I perform many miracles. I tell you that true joy is not in all those things."

"But what is true joy?"

"I am returning from Perugia and I am coming here at night, in the dark. It is winter time and wet and muddy and so cold that icicles form at the edges of my habit and keep striking my legs, and blood flows from such wounds. And I come to the gate, all covered with mud and cold and ice, and after I have knocked and called for a long time, a friar comes and asks: 'Who are you?' I answer: 'Brother Francis.' And he says: 'Go away. This is not a decent time to be going about. You can't come in.'

"And when I insist again, he replies: 'Go away. You are a simple and uneducated fellow. From now on don't stay with us any more. We are so many and so important that we don't need you.'

"But I still stand at the gate and say: 'For the love of God, let me come in tonight.' And he answers: 'I won't.'

"I tell you that if I kept patience and was not upset—that is true joy and true virtue and the salvation of the soul."

—*Little Flowers of St. Francis*

HERE WE ARE AT LAST: THE SECRET OF PERFECT JOY. BUT THE KEY text that serves as our mirror is so strange that our initial response might well be one of exasperation or even revulsion. Perfect joy consists in responding with equanimity to abuse and betrayal? *That's* where all this has been leading? Depending on our temperament, we're likely to shrug our shoulders at what we take to be its lack of bite, or snort in revulsion at what we see as its unseemly masochism, or shudder at what seems its madness. (There's that word again!)

The problem with all these interpretations, however, is that they read *joy* as a response—a reaction to a particular stimulus—although it's perfectly plain from the text that Francis doesn't intend the word in this way. Perfect joy, he tells Brother Leo, isn't an emotional response to good news about fame or success or glory: True joy doesn't consist in any of these. Francis has already liberated himself from the need for external and internal possessions.

Moreover, the story's punch line, where Francis tells the undoubtedly perplexed Leo that joy is possible even in the face of scorn and cruelty, only underscores the fact that he doesn't think of joy as a response. It surely would be masochistic for Francis to see joy as an appropriate reaction to this harsh kind of treatment!

So what's his point? If perfect joy isn't an emotional response, just what is it?

Given this anecdote from the life of Francis, as well as everything we've already noted about freedom and love, I believe it's best to understand Francis's joy as a state of being—a soul-attitude, if you will—that comes if we maximize, with God's help, our potential to be complete. When this happens, we enter squarely into that way of being for which we were created. We become transparent, as it were, and in our newly found clarity, God is able to flow through us. Then we're united in spirit with Spirit, conformed to the God in whose image we're made. We love in and with and through his Spirit, celebrating the wondrous precarity of the world, trusting the Creator's wisdom, and affirming existence, even when events occur that are painful.

To put it in more conventional church language, we experience perfect joy when we are in a state of grace. And we prepare ourselves for the infusion of grace that brings perfect joy when we cultivate the freedom from fear offered by Lady Poverty, Holy Simplicity, and Gracious Humility.

To dwell in joy, to be so identified with God that one is suffused with divine grace, is to see the world in something of the way that God sees it. An old Greek Orthodox tradition has it that when God looks at creation he sees only the good. This is because God is supremely real and supremely good, and hence impervious to the void that evil is.

When we enter into perfect joy, we likewise see the good—the God—in everything around us. Are we cold and hungry, weary and wounded? Do our requests for assistance go unanswered? Are we mocked and insulted? Even though we may suffer, we still see only good and God in all these tribulations because grace allows us to see with God's eye. And to see only good and God is to be overjoyed, even in the midst of pain.

The soul sings, the feet dance, the spirit soars. Foolish? Of course. The foolishness of Christ, of *theia mania*, the madness of a soul that has come into its own and no longer fears, of a soul that celebrates even its tribulations and infirmities as part of God's wondrous plan.

This is perfect joy.

For Reflection

The next time you're in a situation that annoys you, make an effort to step outside of your irritation long enough to catch a glimpse of the deep truth that both you and the situation are part of God's creation. Of course this won't be perfect joy, but it may give you some idea of what lies in store for the person gifted with this state of grace.

MEDITATION

How much joy I have had from the brothers who were the most simple, the most transparent. I would have wished the whole congregation to be like them, for I understood that to overcome Satan and the world it was they who were the best soldiers.

—Carlo Carretto, *I, Francis*

CHAPTER SEVENTEEN

~ Icy Embraces ~

Francis's Words

Often when blessed Francis was honored and people said, "This man is a saint," he would respond to such expressions by saying: "I'm still not sure that I won't have sons and daughters!"

—*The Assisi Compilation*

Mirror

One night Francis felt a grave temptation of the flesh, provoked by him whose very breath will set coals aflame. The moment he felt it coming...he opened the door and went out into the garden where he rolled naked in the deep snow. After that he gathered up some of it with both hands and made seven heaps with it and stood before them, saying to his body, "Look the big one here is your wife and those four are your children, two boys and two girls. The other two are the servants you need to look after them, a man and a woman. And now hurry up and find clothes for them—they are dying of cold. But if all the trouble it takes to look after them is too much for you, then keep your services for God alone."

—Bonaventure, *Life of St. Francis*

ONE OF THE WORST FAILINGS OF RELIGION IS SYRUPY PIETY. MANY people who turn away from Christianity do so because they simply can't stomach the mindlessly happy-face attitude they encounter in bad books or sermons on spirituality. They sense, and correctly so, that they're being flimflammed. In the real world, people hurt, hearts break, and children suffer, and all the feel-good devotional tracts ever printed can't whitewash that.

The last thing in the world we want to do, then, is to fall into the trap of confusing Francis's perfect joy with pseudoreligious feel-goodism. As I emphasized in the previous chapter, joy is a state of being, *not* an emotion. It's entirely possible to *be* joyful without actually *feeling* particularly happy. For most of us, in fact, it's the more common situation.

Loving and celebrating from the fullness of a grace-suffused soul doesn't mean we won't suffer. It *does* mean, however, that we somehow manage to discern the presence of God behind the suffering.

The story of Francis and his snow family is a case in point. It's a heartbreaking tale if you read between the lines. Prim and proper old Bonaventure only intends it to be a warning against sexual lust—temptations of the flesh—and thus comes dangerously close to spooning up some pious treacle. But it takes little reflection to realize that the story, more profoundly, is an expression of the bitter and bone-deep loneliness that sometimes afflicted Francis.

In following the path of poverty and dedicating himself to the service of God and humankind, Francis renounced the opportunity for the more exclusive kind of love that a husband and father feels for his family. The sacrifice was an essential stage along his personal path (although, as he himself frequently insisted, not necessarily along *everyone's* spiritual path). Given his temperament and personality, it was an essential strategy in his breaking through to the freedom that brings joy. Still, he felt the sacrifice keenly at times, and then the pain of his isolation was so bitter that he would seek small consolation by embracing icy images of family members he would never have in the flesh.

But in the midst of his despair, he discerned the presence of God: *Take care to serve one Master!* Whether we feel merry or forlorn, God is in our midst, working through our souls. At the end of the day, that's all that matters.

The story of Francis and the snow family also reminds us of a point we've already noticed: the precarity of existence. Humans, you recall, are amphibious creatures, with one foot in the physical world and the other foot in the spiritual world. It only stands to reason that all of us—even those who have attained the soul-attitude of joy, even saints like Francis—will oscillate from time to time, swinging back and forth between episodes of light and darkness (yet another reason for taking the virtue of Gracious Humility seriously). Even when the pendulum throws us into a dark night, God is present and joy is possible.

Finally, this little story repeats a spiritual warning taught by all the saints: When it comes to religion, we ought not to allow ourselves to become obsessed with the desire for what are usually called "sweet consolations." Many Christians gauge their spiritual states by their emotional ones, mistakenly presuming that if they feel happy or serene, they must be right with God.

There are several obvious dangers in this way of thinking. One is that it ignores what we've already noted: Perfect joy is an abiding state of being rather than a fleeting emotional response. Another is that a mania for religious consolation makes us especially susceptible to feel-good piety that may be emotionally satisfying but is spiritually empty. A third danger is that we too quickly assume we've been abandoned by God, and hence fall into despair and recrimination, once our good mood passes. Our amphibious nature keeps us oscillating enough as it is, without adding the instability of emotion to the mix.

When one weighs the alternatives, there are worse things than an occasional icy embrace.

FOR REFLECTION
Do you tend to gauge your spiritual health by whether or not you feel happy or content? If so, could you be confusing spiritual joy with mere emotional response?

MEDITATION
We know that joy is the sweetness of contact with the love of God, that affliction is the wound of this same contact when it is painful, and that only the contact matters, not the manner of it.

—Simone Weil, *The Simone Weil Reader*

CHAPTER EIGHTEEN

~ Singing in French ~

FRANCIS'S WORDS

The Lord who consoles the afflicted has never left me without consolation. For behold, I who could not hear the lutes of men have heard a far sweeter lute.

—Thomas of Celano, *Second Life of Francis*

MIRROR

Sometimes Francis would act in the following way. When the sweetest melody of spirit would bubble up in him, he would give exterior expression to it in French, and the breath of the divine whisper which his ear perceived in secret would burst forth in French in a song of joy. At times, as we saw with our own eyes, he would pick up a stick from the ground and putting it over his left arm, would draw across it, as across a violin, a little bow bent by means of a string; and going through the motions of playing, he would sing in French about his Lord.

—Thomas of Celano, *Second Life of Francis*

IN OUR RESOLVE TO AVOID THINKING OF PERFECT JOY AS NOTHING more than mawkish feel-goodism, we ought not to forget that it can also be an occasion for great merriment. Pope John XXIII wisely noted that a gloomy Christian is a bad Christian, an obser-vation that ought to be taken to heart by those who take a perverse satisfaction in dwelling on the wretched sinfulness of humanity. The closer one comes to God, the source of love, all good things, and laughter, the more merry one generally ought to be.

For an individual who's received the grace of perfect joy and entered into the new soul-attitude that trustingly affirms being, God is always close, even during those lonely snow-swept times when he feels far away. How could one not leap heavenward and shout hosannas in sheer delight when hearing the "sweetest melody of spirit"?

Francis was a lover of music from way back. Wandering troubadours would visit Assisi to croon their ballads and love songs, and young Francis would listen in rapture for hours on end. We've already seen that as an adult he sometimes referred to himself as God's knight. Just as frequently he liked to call himself God's troubadour.

The life he led was his ballad of praise. Everywhere he went, he sang of the beauty of divine love. But sometimes he was so full of this Love that he had to cut capers or risk exploding. Then he would burst out in extempore song and play makeshift instruments made from branches or stones. The language he used in these fits of ecstasy was Provençal, the language of love, the heartbreakingly melodious language of the traveling troubadours and minstrels.

For centuries and centuries, humans believed that the entire universe was held together by melody—the "music of the spheres"— and that genuine wisdom and inner peace were attainable if one could only sensitize one's heart to the celestial strains. Our cynical age dismisses this ancient lore as superstition. But perhaps we rush to judgment. Music, after all, is essentially harmony; point and counterpoint are juxtaposed in such a way that melody arises from what, considered separately, are dissonant and even discordant notes.

Surely the same thing can be said of the marvelously intricate but cohesive cosmos in which we dwell, a cosmos that, when all is said and done, is as stunningly beautiful as music. And if the universe is a grand composition in which each part mellifluously harmonizes with all others, then there is indeed a music of the spheres that flows in and through existence, that bears the distinctive stamp of the great composer. When our souls thrill to music of any kind, it's because they're reminded of the grand symphony of creation, the music that not only holds the world together but also sounds deep in our hearts. And when we respond, what better way to do so than by adding our voices to the chorus?

FOR REFLECTION

When was the last time you burst into song because you were giddy with happiness? If it's been a while, ask yourself why. The music is always there. Why haven't you been hearing it?

MEDITATION

Here we will sit, and let the sounds of music
Creep in our ears; soft stillness and the night
Become the touches of sweet harmony....

There's not the smallest orb which thou behold'st
But in his motion like an angel sings....
Such harmony is in immortal souls...

—William Shakespeare, *The Merchant of Venice*

CHAPTER NINETEEN

~ Celebrating Others ~

FRANCIS'S WORDS

We have been called to heal wounds, to unite what has fallen apart, and to bring home those who have lost their way.

—*The Legend of the Three Companions*

MIRROR

Once the mother of two of the brothers came to the saint confidently asking an alms. The holy father had pity on her and said to his vicar, Brother Peter of Catania: "Can we give some alms to our mother?" Francis was accustomed to call the mother of any brother his mother and the mother of all the brothers. Brother Peter answered him: "There is nothing left in the house that could be given her." And he added: "We have one New Testament from which we read the lessons at Matins since we do not have a breviary." Blessed Francis said to him: "Give the New Testament to our mother that she might sell it to take care of her needs, since we are admoished by it to help the poor. I believe indeed that the gift of it will be more pleasing to God than our reading from it."

—Thomas of Celano, *Second Life of Francis*

PERFECT JOY IS AN AFFIRMATION AND CELEBRATION OF BEING— the being of creation, and the Being of the Creator. Awe for the one leads to reverence for the other. Bonaventure often wrote that all creation is stamped with the footprints of God. Knowing how to read the book of nature leads one inexorably back to the book's Author.

We are those parts of creation most distinctively imprinted with the Maker's seal. We are made in the image of God. This can only mean that we have Godlike spiritual qualities (God, after all, can't be said to have blue or brown eyes, or straight or curly hair!), and it's precisely these qualities that we consciously embrace when we affirm being.

What makes us unique images of God is our potential for love, for compassion, for kindness, for self-surrender and even self-sacrifice. What makes us images of God is our capacity—one of God's greatest gifts to us—to empty ourselves in order to make room for others.

How do we best celebrate our own and others' humanity? Not, as the world believes, by building monuments to great men and women, or by falling into a shallow humanism that lauds humans as the measures of all things. This isn't celebration so much as idolatry.

A Christian celebration of humanity consists in lovingly midwifing our fellow humans into full being. One of our God-given endowments is creativity, the ability to cooperate with God in the inauguration of the kingdom. We're called to use this creativity in nurturing our brothers and sisters as full members of that kingdom, and we do this by going out of our way to help them recognize and affirm themselves as images of God.

In concrete terms, this means performing the acts of charity listed in the twenty-fifth chapter of Matthew: clothing the naked, tending the sick, visiting the imprisoned, giving food and drink to the hungry and thirsty. Celebrating the sheer existence of others often demands that we do the dirty work of easing the material burdens that inhibit them from arriving at a conscious appreciation of their own holiness.

Above all else, we need to avoid the pseudoaffirmation of spiritual ministration that ignores physical pain and want. This kind of pie-in-the-sky Christianity has been justly criticized by those outside the faith. It's also contrary to both the spirit of the Scriptures and the actual example set for us by Christ. A love that worries about the state of another's soul without doing anything concrete to ease material suffering is an easy and cheap facsimile of genuine love.

Francis knew this well, and energetically warned his brothers against settling for cheap love. The story that serves as our mirror in this chapter wonderfully illustrates a celebration of humans that refuses to indulge in cheap love. Francis's point is that even though sacred Scripture is indeed holy—he was famous for reverencing even old scraps of paper on which the word *God* was written— the poorest and lowliest human is even more so, necessarily taking priority when it comes to nurturance.

What we do to the least of humans we do to Christ himself because each and every one of us is imbued with the spirit of Christ. To celebrate humans is to work for the release and flourishing of the divine Spirit within every heart. Moreover, what we do to the least of humans we do also to ourselves, because all of us are made one in spirit by the indwelling Christ.

True celebration of humans doesn't distinguish between "mine" and "thine." All of us are united into the eternal community, the body of Christ, that pulsating core of energy that nudges creation ever closer to fulfillment.

FOR REFLECTION

First John says that we can hardly be expected to love and celebrate the invisible God if we're incapable of genuinely loving and celebrating the brothers and sisters in whose midst we dwell (see 1 John 4:20). The implication is that no one can legitimately claim to love God who doesn't likewise love others—and this love must express itself in concrete ways. Take a look at your own life and ask yourself whether you truly celebrate humans and love God.

MEDITATION

The one principle of hell is—"I am my own."

—George MacDonald

CHAPTER TWENTY

~ Celebrating Sister Mother Earth ~

FRANCIS'S WORDS

All praise be yours, my Lord, through Sister Earth, our mother,
  Who feeds us in her sovereignty and produces
  Various fruits with colored flowers and herbs.

—The Canticle of Brother Sun

MIRROR

Everything found its way into Francis's brotherhood, because everything came forth from the hands of God the Creator, who is Love. Francis enrolled the sun and extended his domain to the last blade of grass and the least of the insects.

—Julien Green, God's Fool

I MENTIONED IN THE LAST CHAPTER THAT BONAVENTURE THE theologian argued that all of physical reality is stamped with evidence of the Creator. Francis, of course, was no theologian. We've already noted his uneasiness with an overabundance of head learning and an underabundance of heart loving. But he shared and, more importantly, lived Bonaventure's intuition.

For Francis, the beauty of nature constantly whispered, "God." It's not beyond the mark to claim, as certain commentators have, that Francis thought of nature as God's body. In celebrating the beauty of fields and vineyards, birds and beasts, wind and sunshine, and snow and rain, Francis joyfully affirmed the ever-abiding presence of divine beauty on and in earth. It's no wonder that Pope John Paul II proclaimed him the patron saint of environmentalists.

But we need to be extremely careful with the word *environment*. Had Francis ever used the term, he would have meant something quite different from what many people intend today. When we speak of "the environment," we typically mean "surroundings," a space that we occupy but aren't essentially connected to. We presume that we're *in* but not *of* our environment, and this in turn reflects a fundamental attitude common in the West since at least the eighteenth century: that the environment is foreign, other-than-us, thing-like, and it consequently can be manipulated howsoever we please.

How, we ask, could any reasonable person presume that humans have moral (much less religious!) obligations to trees or stones or weather or even animals? They're just things in our thing-filled environment. So we grant ourselves license to do with them what we will. Normally, the only line we draw when it comes to manipulating "the environment" is our own self-interest—or, what we *perceive* to be our self-interest.

This isn't Francis's understanding of the environment at all. He felt, as deeply as he ever felt anything, that all nature is bound together by Spirit in such an intimately inseparable way that every member of nature is akin to all others. His affection for his natural kindred wasn't limited to bunnies or beautiful birds, even though popular imagination has domesticated his wild and profligate love in countless backyard statues and birdbaths.

His ardor extended to all of nature, so he could say—and *mean*—that the sun and fire and wind were his brothers, the moon and water and earth his sisters. Even stranger to our contemporary way of thinking, he dared to affectionately refer to Death, another natural phenomenon, as his Sister.

One doesn't just treat members of one's family lovingly; one also treats them with respect. The tales of Francis's respectful concern for nature are legion. Even those persons who have no special affinity with him find them charming and sometimes inspiring.

Francis never liked to douse a fire with water, for example, because he saw it as an infliction of unnecessary violence on both Brother Fire and Sister Water. Once when he sat too close to an open hearth and his robe caught on fire, he chastised his panicked brothers, who quickly patted out the flame and mourned the death of Brother Fire, who after all had only wished to embrace him. When the other brothers grumbled about intemperate weather, Francis sang praises to his sisters Rain and Snow and Sleet. Truly, nothing in nature was foreign to Francis. He was *of* his environment as a son or daughter is *of* his or her family.

We who tend to think of nature as nothing more than a usable commodity can learn a great deal from Francis's relationship with the environment. He teaches us the liberating truth that our physical surroundings are holy because they aren't *purely* physical. Instead, they're permeated through and through with the Spirit and beauty of God. In a mysterious way that the mind can't fathom but the heart knows full well, we don't just dwell in God's world. In dwelling in God's world, we also abide in God himself.

For Reflection

In his "Canticle of the Creatures," Francis tells us that Sister Mother Earth both sustains and governs us. Even though most of us may have no difficulty with the notion that the earth sustains us, the claim that she also governs us could be startling. We typically fancy that it's we who govern the earth. Reflect prayerfully on Francis's reversal. What significance does it have for your life?

Meditation

This world is pregnant with God!

—Angela of Foligno, *Memorial*

CHAPTER TWENTY-ONE

~ Celebrating God ~

FRANCIS'S WORDS

Almighty, most high and supreme God, Father, holy and just, Lord, King of heaven and earth, we give you thanks for yourself.

—*The Rule of 1221*

MIRROR

Looking up to Heaven and raising his hands, he prayed with intense fervor and devotion, saying: "My God and my all!"... Until matins he said nothing but "My God and my all!"

—*The Little Flowers of Saint Francis*

WHAT I'M GOING TO SAY HERE IS BOUND TO STARTLE SOME AND rile others, but here it goes: Many of us who *claim* to believe in God actually *don't*. This includes lots of people who faithfully attend church or regularly read spiritual books like this one or talk about God at every available opportunity.

Now that I've risked offending you, let me explain.

Our beliefs come in all shapes and sizes. I believe, for example, that I have a gray beard, that Wales borders on England, that most pants have pockets, that the sun will rise in the east tomorrow morning, and that my family loves me. I'm confident that every one of these beliefs is most likely true, but I'm also confident that they aren't equally important.

The belief that I happen to have a beard, while true, is relatively insignificant when compared to my belief about the sun's rising tomorrow. Moreover, if I find out next week that my understanding of modern fashion is hopelessly outdated and that most pants *don't* have pockets, I won't be nearly as shocked as I would be to discover that my belief about my family's love is false. In the grand scheme of things, nobody much cares whether pants have pockets, but everybody wants to be loved.

The general rule here is that our emotional investment in our beliefs is proportionate to the weight of their content. Most of our beliefs are relatively unimportant to us. They hover on the periphery of our experience, we rarely call upon them, and if we discover that one or two of them are in fact false, it's no big deal. But a handful of our beliefs are quite important to us. We rely on them each day of our lives, and our world would rock if we discovered them to be false.

Now, consider belief in God. If God exists, then by definition nothing is more *real* than God or more *vital* for our own existence. As the theologians say, the existence of everything else depends on God, but God's existence depends on nothing. It follows that no belief we could possibly hold ought to be more *important for us* than our belief in God.

Belief in God isn't just another belief about just another fact in the world. It stands in a class of its own, and if we hold it, it should be the one belief that's absolutely central, the belief upon which all our other beliefs ultimately rest, the one that serves as the foundation for all our behavior in the world. We may be able to endure giving up any and all of our other beliefs—even big ones like the sun rising in the east tomorrow—but our belief in God ought to be so central to our emotional well-being that to give it up would be to die.

Yet look at the way things really are. How many people who say they believe in God hold that conviction as the central one of their lives? Not many, unfortunately. All their other beliefs, not to mention actions, don't orbit around their belief in God. Instead, their belief in God too often is just another peripheral opinion they could do without if push came to shove. Other beliefs usurp its primacy: belief in themselves, in a cause, in a loved one, in the value of money, and so on.

All this can be squeezed into a simple formula: If you claim to believe in God, but your belief isn't the most important one in your life, the one belief that you couldn't survive without, then you're just fooling yourself. You don't really believe in God at all.

These are harsh words, but ones that Francis would want us to heed. The reason is this: Unless one truly believes in God, one is incapable of genuinely celebrating God.

An observer once watched as Francis prayed throughout the length of an entire night. To his amazement, Francis spent the whole time simply repeating, over and over, "My God and my all! My God and my all!"

This simple act, so undramatic, so seemingly modest, in fact was an incredibly intense celebration. Francis truly believed that God was all, and he realized that the only celebration worthy of God is wonder-filled and grateful acknowledgment of God's allness. Pageantry and pomp and circumstance aren't needed to celebrate the living God. All that's required is the heartfelt conviction that nothing—absolutely nothing—is more real or important. When we reach this point (*if* we reach this point) our belief in God is a simultaneous celebration of God.

Which is exactly how things should be.

For Reflection

Look deeply into the mirror Francis holds up before you in this chapter, and ask yourself, perhaps for the first time in your life, this question: Do I really believe in God?

Meditation

The French philosopher and mathematician Blaise Pascal scrawled the words on the following page on a bit of paper immediately after a mystical encounter with the ultimate reality of God. He sewed the paper into his clothes and wore it next to his heart for the rest of his life.

God of Abraham, God of Isaac, God of Jacob,
not of philosophers and scholars.
Certainty, certainty, heartfelt joy, peace.
God of Jesus Christ.
God of Jesus Christ.
My God and your God.

Thy God shall be my God.

The world forgotten, and everything except God.

Jesus Christ.

Jesus Christ.

Amen.

—Blaise Pascal, *Pensees*

CHAPTER TWENTY-TWO

~ What to Do with Brother Body? ~

FRANCIS'S WORDS

While we are bound to avoid over-indulgence in food, which injures both body and soul, we must also avoid excessive abstinence, especially as the Lord desires mercy, and not sacrifice.

—*A Mirror of Perfection*

MIRROR

Francis continually mortified his body most harshly, not only when he was well, but also when he was ill. Seldom indeed did he relax this severity; so much so, that on his deathbed he confessed to having sinned grievously against Brother Body.

—*The Legend of the Three Companions*

EVEN SAINTS MAKE MISTAKES. AND FRANCIS MADE A DOOZY, ONE he finally confessed and regretted only at the very end of his life. It had to do with his body.

Francis was notorious in his own day—and even more so in ours—for the physical punishments he inflicted on himself. After his conversion, he convinced himself that "Brother Body" (or, as he sometimes said, "Brother Ass") was a strong-headed and feral beast that would lead him into mischief if not subdued. The tired and chaffed skin clamored continuously for warm clothing, strong shoes, and a nice hot bath. The ravenous belly craved oven-fresh bread, ripe olives, and fragrant cheese, and perhaps even a mouthful of wine every now and then.

And the frustrated burning below the belly? Best not even to think about *that*. Perdition lay in that direction.

Francis felt as if he couldn't trust his own body, that it was a highly charged dynamo of desires and lusts that would explode with megaton force if he ever loosened his iron grip on it. For him, the pernicious thing about bodily desire is that all it needs is a tiny foothold to conquer the soul. Giving in to a single urge, no matter how trivial it might seem at the time, opened the floodgates. Before you quite knew what was happening, you succumbed to lusts that mired you in filth and exiled you from God.

Francis's solution was to beat his body into submission. He fasted more than he supped, and when he did eat, he scooped up ashes and salted his food with them. He spent most of his nights in prayer, allowing himself only three or four hours of sleep. He exhausted his passions by laboring mightily in fields and trudging long distances on mountain roads. And he punished his flesh for any waywardness it might still have left by rolling in thorny brambles or jumping in ditches of slushy snow.

Constant vigilance was his watchword. The slightest twinge of bodily desire had to be ruthlessly suppressed.

If there's a single thing most likely to repel a modern-day reader of Francis's life, it's this extreme asceticism. There's good reason that it grates on us: Francis was wrong to torture poor Brother Body so.

His failure to understand this until he lay dying was a grave blind spot in his spiritual vision. Even as he celebrated other people and the world of nature, even as he joyfully affirmed all being for the sake of its Creator, he treated his own body as if it were a mortal enemy. But of course the body isn't the enemy. It's created by God, and as such is good. How could flesh be vile when God-in-Christ himself gladly wore it?

Treat the body with respect, therefore, not contempt. Feed it properly, clothe it decently, and see to it that Brother Ass, who after all graciously consents to carry us around all our days, enjoys the simple pleasures of rest and food and drink. And if one has no special calling to celibacy, then celebrate also the body's talent for marital lovemaking. This, too, is an affirmation of being, not an act to be despised and feared.

It's remarkable that Francis had so much love to give to others, but spared none for his own body. We know that he refused to hold the other brothers up to the same harsh standards he imposed on himself. Once in the middle of the night, as the brothers lay sleeping at la Portiuncula, a faint voice cried out: "I'm dying! I'm dying!" Quickly lighting a candle, Francis discovered that the moan came from a brother who was weak and ill from excessive fasting. There and then Francis lit a fire and cooked the man food, gently chastising him for his ascetical severity.

Even more remarkably, Francis ate with the famished brother in order to spare him humiliation. Mercy always trumped rules and regulations when it came to Francis's dealings with others. But he simply didn't see that he owed the same loving compassion to his own flesh until it was too late to do anything more than beg Brother Body's pardon for years of ill-treatment.

Remember: We humans are amphibians, oscillating between the urges of our physical nature and the aspirations of our spiritual nature. The point of the spiritual journey isn't to destroy our physical nature—our body, if you will—because doing so would be to run counter to what we are. Our proper goal is to train the body so that its urges harmonize with our noblest spiritual ideals in celebration of the wondrous world in which God has graciously placed us.

Brother Body is an essential part of who we are, and to torture him is to torture ourselves. It's also to do shameful violence to one of God's beloved creatures. God grant that we learn this truth long before we lie on our deathbeds.

FOR REFLECTION

Have you made peace with Brother Body? Or do you tend to view it as a more-or-less shameful partner to whom you're chained? Do you wear your flesh joyfully or guiltily?

MEDITATION

Do you not know that your body is a temple of the Holy Spirit within you, which you have from God, and that you are not your own? For you were bought with a price; therefore glorify God in your body.

—1 Corinthians 6:19–20

CHAPTER TWENTY-THREE

~ Becoming Prayer ~

FRANCIS'S WORDS

When a servant of God is praying and is visited by a new consolation from the Lord, he should, before he comes away from his prayer, raise his eyes to heaven and with hands joined say to the Lord: "This consolation and sweetness you have sent from heaven, Lord, to me, an unworthy sinner, and I return it to you so you may keep it for me, for I am a robber of your treasure."

—Thomas of Celano, *Second Life of Francis*

MIRROR

All his attention and affection he directed with his whole being to the one thing which he was asking of the Lord, not so much praying as becoming himself a prayer.

—Thomas of Celano, *Second Life of Francis*

CONTRARY TO WHAT MANY PEOPLE THINK, PRAYER IS, OR AT LEAST ought to be, the easiest thing in the world. All we need do is listen with quiet and loving alertness, directing all our "attention and affection," as Thomas of Celano tells us, to the silent voice of God. When prayer works, our entire being flows toward and into God. Then prayer isn't an act that we perform so much as what we *are*. *We* become the prayer, the oblation, the praise and gratitude and openness that we offer to God.

If we fail to pray well—much less to become a living prayer—there are several possible explanations. We may not be attending *lovingly*, for example. Our prayer may be indifferently mechanical, a pro forma ritual in which our hearts aren't really invested.

Or, our prayer may be too noisy, chatty, too full of words. When this happens, we're not able to listen to God for the simple reason that we're too busy talking.

We may even be so fixated on the proper technique for prayer that we don't actually get down to doing it effectively. Our preoccupation with how we pray makes us forgetful of why we pray.

What we need to know is that we already have everything we need to pray effectively. The Spirit of God already dwells within us at our deepest core. When we empty ourselves of ego and distractions and open ourselves to that Spirit—when we longingly and lovingly listen to him—we *enter* into a state of prayer. When we've become so receptive to the indwelling Spirit that we ceaselessly attend to him throughout our daily activities, we *become* a living prayer.

One of the younger brothers once asked Francis for permission to own a breviary. Francis's response is startling and revealing. He shouted out to the youngster: "I *am* a breviary! I *am* a breviary!" This is not the utterance of a megalomaniac, but rather of a God-filled person who realizes that once one becomes a living prayer, one no longer needs devotional aids such as prayer books. All one needs to pray is God, and God is always present. This is the truth Francis hoped to impress on the youth.

So much for attention in prayer. But affection, or love, must not be neglected. In fact, the importance of love in prayer can't be overstated.

Ordinary experience teaches us that we're more likely to listen closely to loved ones than to mere acquaintances or strangers. Love provides the staying power to sit quietly and open oneself to the beloved. In fact, love makes being in the presence of the beloved a sheer joy, an act to which we long to return again and again. Cold intellectual curiosity, much less a mechanical sense of religious obligation, is incapable of sustaining the alert attentiveness necessary for genuine prayer.

In the final analysis, then, an inability to pray well is an inability to love well. Conversely, a person who loves well continuously prays, even if he or she rarely does so in a formal, ritualistic way. This is because the heart of prayer is expressed in the Great Commandment: Love God with all your heart and mind and soul (see Matthew 22:36–40). When one lives in this way—prays in this way—one joyfully affirms and gratefully embraces the great gift of being. The person of genuine prayer, the person who becomes a living breviary, is inescapably a person of great and perfect joy.

FOR REFLECTION
Have you ever felt as if you were a living breviary? Reflect on the experience, trying to recapture the circumstances.

MEDITATION
Prayer is not a way of being busy with God instead of with people. In fact, it unmasks the illusion of busyness, usefulness,

and indispensability. It is a way of being empty and useless in the presence of God and so of proclaiming our basic belief that all is grace and nothing is simply the result of hard work.

—Henri Nouwen, *The Living Reminder*

CHAPTER TWENTY-FOUR

~ Wisdom ~

FRANCIS'S WORDS

A religious has been killed by the letter when he has no desire to follow the spirit of Sacred Scripture, but wants to know what it says only so that he can explain it to others. On the other hand, those have received life from the spirit of Sacred Scripture who, by their words and example, refer to the most high God, to whom belongs all good, all that they know or wish to know, and do not allow their knowledge to become a source of self-complacency.

—Admonitions

MIRROR

Francis was not an experienced teacher, but he had no lack of knowledge, so that he was able to resolve doubtful questions and bring all their implications to light. There is nothing strange in the fact that he should have been enlightened by God to understand the Scriptures; by his perfect conformity with Christ he practiced the truths which are contained in them and carried their Author in his heart by the abundant infusion of the Holy Spirit.

—Bonaventure, *Life of St. Francis*

WE LIVE IN A DAY AND AGE THAT PUTS A HIGH PREMIUM ON information. Most of us are ravenous consumers of facts, and we judge ourselves and others as smart in terms of how many we have under our belts. I suspect that's one of the reasons computers have become common household appliances. Our mania for facts is appeased by cyberspace's astounding ability to feed us all the data we could ever want.

No one would deny that factual information is important. It's difficult to see how we could survive long in our world without it. But we harm ourselves if we presume that factual information is the sum total of knowledge, and that we can rest contentedly after stopping at it. This presumption not only breeds a certain arrogance, which supposes that mere command of data makes one superior to others—the "Trivial Pursuit" or "Jeopardy" sort of snobbery. It also encourages the error that being wise amounts to nothing more than having an encyclopedia of facts lodged away in one's memory.

Spiritually speaking, life is more complicated than this. Wisdom isn't a function of how many facts one knows or even how smart one is. Wisdom isn't book learning (although it's not necessarily incompatible with it), and the wise person certainly doesn't lord his or her learning over others. Wisdom, instead, consists in being receptive to truth, and then living the truth that one receives.

We can better understand this if we consider the ancient Greek word for truth, the word that the Gospel writers themselves used: *aletheia*. *Aletheia* is difficult to translate, but it can be rendered as "unveiling," "unconcealing," or even "revealing." The implication is that truth is an unconcealing or a revealing of what was previously hidden.

To know the truth is to look beneath the surface of things and discern the treasure concealed therein. When one does, something happens that goes far beyond adding another piece of information to one's collection. A transformation takes place: The truth that's been revealed changes the person who chances upon it.

A person who has penetrated to *aletheia* henceforth *abides* in the truth, and in doing so becomes a beacon of truth for others. In short, he or she attains wisdom: a living, penetrating, and imparting participation in truth. According to Bonaventure, this attainment is an infusion from the Holy Spirit.

Bonaventure tells us that Francis achieved this level of wisdom. Even though he was "not an experienced teacher," he was full of wisdom, able to shed light on difficult or doubtful questions. What enabled Francis to do this? Bonaventure's response is revealing: "his imitation of Christ."

Francis's wisdom came from holy living rather than a life of secluded study. He discovered hidden truth not by going off in pursuit of facts, but by living as Christ lived. Perhaps now it's even more clear why Francis's devotion to Holy Simplicity led him to distrust the scholarly ambitions of his more bookish brothers.

We've noted in previous chapters that the imitation of Christ involves a radical yea-saying to being, which in turn spills over into profligate love and deep, deep prayer. Affirming God's creation in love and prayer opens the heart to the divine mystery that lies at the core of things. It may not be easy to express this revelation in words, regardless of how skilled one is in the use of language.

The greatest truths, after all, can be experienced and lived but only haltingly uttered. How difficult it is for the lover to say what's in his or her heart! But for all that, truth *can* be communicated by our actions in the world, and indeed, this is the most effective of all communications. When we become wise—when we open ourselves to the presence of God and lovingly hold the teacher in our hearts—then we display in our activity the perfect truth that we've discovered.

FOR REFLECTION

Could it be that your hunger for information leaves you too preoccupied to have any time for wisdom?

MEDITATION

Then Jesus said to the Jews who had believed in him, "If you continue in my word, you are truly my disciples; and you will know the truth, and the truth will make you free."

—John 8:31–32

CHAPTER TWENTY-FIVE

~ Trials ~

FRANCIS'S WORDS

Farewell, all you my sons, in the fear of God, and may you remain in him always, for a very great trial will come upon you and a great tribulation is approaching. Happy will they be who will persevere in the things they have begun; from them future scandals will separate some.

—Thomas of Celano, *First Life of Francis*

MIRROR

Francis was filled with sorrow that some [of the brothers] had left their former works and had forgotten their earlier simplicity after they had found new things. Wherefore he grieved over those who were once intent upon higher things with their whole desire but who had descended to base and vile things, and had left the true joys to roam and wander amid frivolous and inane things in the field of empty freedom. He prayed therefore that God's mercy might free these sons and asked most earnestly that they might be kept in the grace that had been given to them.

—Thomas of Celano, *First Life of Francis*

FRANCIS SUFFERED GREATLY THE LAST FEW YEARS OF HIS LIFE. Brother Body began to crumble from years of harsh asceticism, afflicting Francis with blindness, stomach problems, and weakness. But the physical pain Francis experienced was nothing compared to the spiritual torment he endured as he watched the Order he loved retreat from true devotion to Lady Poverty, Holy Simplicity, and Gracious Humility.

Francis relinquished leadership of the Order as early as 1217 to dedicate himself more fully to prayer and service. He journeyed to the Holy Land in 1219 and 1220 in a futile effort to convert the sultan and bring a peaceful end to the religious war then raging between Muslims and Christians. When he returned to la Portiuncula, he discovered a disturbing new spirit among the brethren.

Under the influence of the Order's new leader, Elias, the brothers had begun to accept gifts of property, build monasteries and chapter houses, seek high appointments in the Church, and teach theology and philosophy at universities—in short, to live exactly the kind of life that Francis saw as self-imprisonment. Over the next few decades, the Franciscans would acquire an unpleasant (and at least partly deserved) reputation for religious hypocrisy: preaching poverty but living high on the hog. No less a poet than Dante would chide them in his *Paradiso* (Canto XI) for their restless gluttony.

The Order eventually recovered its spiritual sense of direction, although even then Francis's own practice of absolute poverty tended to remain more of an ideal for the Order than an actuality. But this recovery occurred only after Francis's death. He went to his grave tortured by the fear that the Brothers had willingly thrown away the freedom and perfect joy his word and example had offered them.

The sorry story of Francis's declining years has more than just historical value. What happened to his Order frequently happens to the individual Christian as well. We find ourselves frightened by the radical freedom God offers us: freedom from enslavement to material possessions, from interior arrogance and jealousy and ambition.

This kind of liberation is too contrary to the ways of the world. If embraced, it takes us out of the social mainstream. So even as we yearn for it in our heart of hearts, we also fear and flee it, usually by convincing ourselves that we can compromise, giving a little here and a little there, in order to get along in the so-called real world.

Christ came to offer genuine liberation and perfect joy to humankind. But most of us, like Francis's brethren, suspect that such liberation is too ideal to be practical and that concessions have to be made if we're to get through the day. Something good and holy inside us doesn't want to settle for anything less than the ideal. But our play-it-safe practical side warns us that we've got to bend if we hope to accomplish anything in this life.

How to live Christ's vision and honor Christ's example in the hurly-burly of everyday life while at the same time being concretely effective? How to navigate between an impractical spiritual purity and a practical lowering of the bar? These questions have troubled every generation since Christ's. They are the trials that any Christian can expect to face at some time or another in his or her life.

For Reflection

Do you sometimes feel as if you've sold out your Christian integrity in your efforts to labor and minister effectively in the world?

Meditation

One night when Blessed Peter Pettinaio of the Third Order was praying in the Cathedral of Siena, he saw Our Lord Jesus Christ enter the church, followed by a great throng of saints. And each time Christ raised his foot, the form of his foot remained imprinted on the ground. And all the saints tried as hard as they could to place their feet in the trace of His footsteps, but none of them was able to do so perfectly. Then Saint Francis came in and set his feet right in the footsteps of Jesus Christ.

—*The Little Flowers of Saint Francis*

CHAPTER TWENTY-SIX

~ Little by Little ~

FRANCIS'S WORDS

Let us begin, brothers, to serve the Lord God, for up until now we have made little or no progress.

—Thomas of Celano, *First Life of Francis*

MIRROR

Francis did not consider that he had laid hold of his goal as yet, and persevering untiringly in his purpose of attaining holy newness of life, he hoped always to make a beginning.

—Thomas of Celano, *First Life of Francis*

ONE STORY ABOUT FRANCIS'S FINAL YEARS IS PARTICULARLY instructive. According to the tale, Francis was in agony over what he saw as the breakdown of both the Order and his own most cherished dreams. As he knelt in unquiet, troubled prayer, beseeching God to show him how to keep things from breaking completely apart, the Lord replied.

Accounts of the event differ, but basically the message was: Who do you think you are, Francis?! Do you really think that the Order rises or falls on your back? I formed the Order through you, and I'll continue it long after you're gone. So don't sweat the big picture. You just do your own bit as best you can, and leave the rest to me.

We ought to remember this response (reminiscent, by the way, of God's answer to Job) as we grapple with the never-ending tussle between our Christian ideals and worldly accommodation. It reminds us of at least three important points.

First, we're finite creatures situated squarely in a world of space and time. Therefore, a certain degree of accommodation is necessary even on God's part. We are the material instruments God uses to bring about the kingdom, and we are limited in power, understanding, and depth. But God joyfully embraces the opportunity to wield these instruments instead of wearily turning his back on the whole enterprise, even though the tools he uses to work his will in the world aren't as perfect as he is.

Second, we likewise must make concessions to the world of space and time in which we dwell. Granted, each of us ought to be on guard against the self-deception of selling out in the name of accommodation. But we should also recognize that our own ideals may not fit everyone equally well, and that what's ultimately important is to love people, not ideals.

St. Paul tells us that he willingly became all things to all persons in order to teach Christ (see 1 Corinthians 9:22). He would talk philosophy with the Greeks, discuss Scripture with the Jews, and eat unclean meats with the pagans, not because he necessarily wished to, but because he realized that such accommodations of his own high standards were necessary to spread the Gospel. In a perfect world, such concessions would be unnecessary.

Similarly, in a perfect world, Francis's ideals of voluntary poverty, simplicity, and humility would remain radical and uncom-promised. But in the world in which we dwell, sometimes a little must be conceded in order to gain a lot.

And third, God is at work even through the worldly concessions and accommodations we're called to make. Failure to realize this could betoken either distrust of God or arrogance. If the first, we refuse to believe that God's providential hand works behind the scenes, or that God knows the big picture while we're privy to only one tiny piece of it. If the second, we fancy ourselves so indispens-able to God and our fellow humans that creation crumbles if our own hopes, dreams, or ideals are thwarted in even the slightest way.

Thomas of Celano says it well: Our goal is "holy newness" and we must begin our efforts for it again and again. Our task is to cooperate with God by bringing to light new fragments of reality that help our brothers and sisters better celebrate the full splendor of God's creation. Whenever we draw their attention to these frag-ments, holy newness enters the world.

These fragments, slender and fragile as they are, can't be manhan-dled. We must hold them up one by one, working patiently, so that little by little the light they refract spreads everywhere. We may despair at the slowness with which holy newness enters the world, just as we may suffer from the fear that we're too accommodating in our efforts to serve God. But then we ought to remember God's message to Francis, trust in his direction, and resolve to play our part, leaving the rest to God.

FOR REFLECTION

What standards do you invoke in your own life to help distinguish between selling out to the world and accommodating the world for the sake of the Gospel?

MEDITATION

We must remind ourselves that, though our lives are small and our acts seem insignificant, we are generative elements of this universe, and we create meaning with each act that we perform or fail to perform.

It is here, on this earth, in the day to day, on the street corners, at our evening table, in the homes of our friends, at the bedside of the sick, in the arms of our wife or husband, in the warmth or sadness of our child's days, that the universe is being formed.

—Kent Nerburn, *Make Me an Instrument of Your Peace*

CHAPTER TWENTY-SEVEN

God-Pierced

FRANCIS'S WORDS

May I feel in my soul and in my body, as much as possible, that pain which You, dear Jesus, sustained in the hour of Your most bitter Passion. May I feel in my heart, as much as possible, that excessive love with which You, O Son of God, were inflamed in willingly enduring such suffering for us sinners.

—The Little Flowers of Saint Francis

MIRROR

While he was still alive, God conferred on Francis the wonderful prerogative of a most singular privilege. Wrapt in divine contemplation, blessed Francis was absorbed in seraphic love and desire; and through the tenderness of his compassion he was transformed into a living crucifix. Thus the inmost desire of his burning love was fulfilled. One morning two years before his death, about the feast of the Exaltation of the Cross, while he was praying on the side of a mountain named La Verna, there appeared to him a seraph in the beautiful figure of a crucified man, having his hands and feet extended as though on a cross, and clearly showing the face of Jesus Christ. Two wings met above his head, two covered the rest of his body to the feet, and two were spread as in flight.

When the vision passed, the soul of Francis was afire with love; and on his body there appeared the wonderful impression of the wounds of our Lord Jesus Christ. Blessed Francis did all in his power to hide these wounds, not wishing that God's gift should be seen by men; but he could not hide this gift entirely, and it became known to his intimate companions. After his death, however, all the brothers who were present saw clearly that his body bore the wounds of Christ in hands and feet.

—*The Legend of the Three Companions*

THE MIRACLE OF THE STIGMATA OCCURRED SOMETIME AROUND September 14, 1224. According to Franciscan tradition, Francis carried the five open wounds of Christ for the rest of his life. Bleeding continuously and ever aching, they caused him agony every time he took a step or held a cup or stretched forth a hand or foot. They also became the capstone of his perfect joy.

How can we understand this mystery?

For eight hundred years now, people have argued over the significance of Francis's stigmata. At one end of the spectrum are those skeptics who insist that the five wounds are psychosomatic manifestations of overwrought emotions. Francis, they contend, had spent a lifetime meditating on the passion and death of Jesus. This morbid fascination, coupled with a body broken by harsh abuse, induced the stigmata.

So the wounds, they say, are really just extreme examples of the power of hysterical autosuggestion. There's nothing miraculous about them. On the contrary, they're pathological in nature.

At the other end of the spectrum are those good folks whose faith is built exclusively upon belief in spectacular miracles: weeping

Madonnas, divine faces on screen doors—and, of course, stigmata. There's no miracle too Hollywoodish for them. Every rumor is accepted at face value as a totally reliable report of an actual event. Nor is there any attempt to read symbolic significance into the reports. The miracles simply are what they appear to be on the surface—in the case of stigmata, a duplication of Christ's wounds and nothing else.

Neither the skeptical nor the true believer approaches can help us understand why the infliction of stigmata upon Francis was actually a gift that capsulated his quest for perfect joy. That's because both of them ignore the deep significance of the event. They fail to look for the symbolic meaning mirrored in the story of the stigmata.

That meaning, I believe, is *love*, and this is what makes the story of Francis's experience on LaVerna so important for those of us who would walk his path.

Francis tried to follow in the footprints of his Master by literally conforming his life in every way to the life of Jesus. Lady Poverty, Holy Simplicity, and Gracious Humility were dear to him only because they were practiced and preached by Jesus.

But these three sacred virtues weren't enough for Francis. Above all else, Jesus's life and ministry expressed itself in complete, sacrificial love, totally liberated from self-interest and jealousy, so exuberantly affirmative of God's creation that it represented the pinnacle of human fulfillment and perfect joy. Francis prayed mightily for the gift of this love, and it was ultimately granted him when he received the stigmata.

The passion of Christ is possible only because of Christ's unbounded love for the world. The passion occurred only because Christ loved creation and God more than himself. Consequently, to love as Christ loved entails suffering as Christ suffered. The two necessarily go hand in hand. This is why Francis found perfect joy in the stigmata—not because of the horrible physical pain it brought, but because of the inflowing of absolute love that pierced his heart even as the mystical iron pierced his limbs and side.

To love as Christ loved, to become more and more Christlike in our actions and thought until only Christ lives in us: This inevitably means suffering because the lover always suffers for the sake of the beloved. But when one has reached this point of the spiritual journey, the suffering is accepted with glad heart and joyous smile.

This is the *real* miracle of the stigmata.

For Reflection

If God offered you the gift of loving as Christ loved, would you have the courage to accept it? What would it look like in your life?

Meditation

Francis always knew where the real miracle lay. It was not in things that happened to his body, though they were wonderful enough. It was the radiance of light and love breaking across the darkness and hate of his world and his time.... Here was a child-like lover of men, ready, if need be, to be crucified for love, but also ready in humble everyday tasks to reveal this love.

—Rufus Jones, *The Luminous Trail*

CHAPTER TWENTY-EIGHT

~ Everyone Has a LaVerna ~

FRANCIS'S WORDS

We are spouses when the faithful soul is joined to our Lord Jesus Christ by the Holy Spirit. We are brothers to Him when we do the will of the Father Who is in heaven. We are mothers, when we carry Him in our heart through divine love and a pure and sincere conscience and when we give birth to Him through His holy manner of working, which should shine before others as an example.

—Earlier Exhortation

MIRROR

Brother John was so simple that he felt bound to do everything that blessed Francis did. When Francis was in a church, the brother wanted to see him and observe him so that he might conform himself to him in all his attitudes; if he genuflected or raised his joined hands in prayer, if he spat or coughed, the brother did the same. Blessed Francis was very amused at this simplicity. Nevertheless, he began to reprimand him. But the other answered: "Father, I promised to do all that you would do; therefore I want to do all that you do." And blessed Francis was in admiration and joy at seeing such purity and simplicity.

—Legend of Perugia

OF ALL THE MEN AND WOMEN WHO FOLLOWED FRANCIS, SIMPLE John is my favorite. Part of the reason is that the stories about him are so funny. I can see him solemnly mimicking every move that Francis makes, and I can see Francis growing more and more irritated by his newly acquired shadow. It's the stuff of vaudeville.

But the main reason I so like Simple John is that I sense common ground between us. Like John, I have to fight constantly the temptation to measure my own spiritual health by how well I imitate others whom I admire. Instead of finding my own road, I tend to want to travel well-marked paths blazed by those who went before me. Instead of striking off on my own and seeing where my feet and the Holy Spirit take me, I waste time scrounging for road maps and travel memoirs.

Yet, for all our points of similarity, John and I differ in one crucial aspect. *My* imitation of saints is sparked for the most part by timidity. *His*, as the *Legend of Perugia* emphasizes, came from the "purity and simplicity" born of faith.

I suspect that many other faint-hearted travelers rely too heavily, as I do, on others' examples. This is ultimately the wrong way. Francis himself knew that his path wasn't for everyone and often steered people who tried to join the First Order toward the Third. He recognized a truth the rest of us should take to heart: There are many ways for the lover to court the Beloved, many different LaVernas.

God awaits us on any number of summits. For a very few, the culmination of their journey is a winged seraph bringing the terrible gift of stigmata. For most others, the culmination is quieter, stiller, gentler. God measures his appearance to suit our temperaments, our talents, and our strength to endure his holy presence.

We're all made in the image of God, but each of us is still his or her own individual person, unique in personality, gifts, and weaknesses. Some of us incline toward the intellectual life while others are more emotional in our orientation to the world. Some of us are introverted, others extroverted. Some are good with their hands, some not so good.

Whatever path we ultimately take to God must be the one that's best suited to the type of person we are. Otherwise, we run the risk of causing ourselves (not to mention others!) extraordinary and quite unnecessary amounts of grief. Slavish imitation of a saint whose way just isn't ours is a sure recipe for disaster—particularly if the primary motivation for our imitation is fear of going it alone.

This doesn't mean that we can't profit from the example of saints such as Francis. He reminds us, for instance, that we ought to cherish the virtues of poverty, simplicity, and humility, even if the way we ultimately live them isn't identical to his own. Francis's example likewise encourages us to break out of our timidity and chart unknown spiritual waters—which, after all, is precisely what he himself did. But at the end of the day, we must take what we can from Francis and then strike out on our own, trusting with as much of Brother John's pure and simple faith as we can possibly muster that God will guide us toward our own LaVerna, our own destiny, our own way of loving, and our own freedom and perfect joy.

For Reflection

The very fact that you're reading this book suggests that you're an admirer of St. Francis. That being the case, ask yourself: Are you inclined to be a Simple John kind of imitator, or are you willing to adapt Francis's spiritual vision creatively to your own life situation?

Meditation

Should the Franciscan tradition teach people to recreate the experience of a Francis or a Clare? Certainly not. The attempt would be fruitless and frustrating.... It continues to be a living tradition today because others have carried on the tradition, in new times and places, in their own words and example. Francis presents us with one example, a moving and inspiring example, but the tradition does not stop with him. In his words, "I have done what was mine to do, may Christ now show you what is yours." Francis wished that his whole life would point to Christ. To stop at Francis would be to frustrate the intention he had for his followers.

—William J. Short, OFM, *Poverty and Joy: The Franciscan Tradition*

CHAPTER TWENTY-NINE

~ Becoming Who You Are ~

FRANCIS'S WORDS

What a man is before God, that he is and no more.

—Admonitions

MIRROR

Bring me out of prison, so that I may give thanks to your name!

—Psalm 142:7

AFTER TWO YEARS OF CARRYING THE STIGMATA, BROTHER BODY, already overburdened with illness, finally gave out. It was autumn 1226. Francis asked to be carried back to his cherished la Portiuncula to die. On his last night he summoned all the brothers at la Portiuncula and, telling them they represented all the Order's members, laid his hands upon them in a final blessing. Then, with his last breaths, Francis recited the words of Psalm 142:7: "Bring me out of prison, that I may give thanks to thy name!"

In part, Francis meant to thank God and Sister Death for delivering him from the prison of a diseased and suffering body. But it's not too much to imagine that he also intended the psalmist's words as a benediction on his entire life. As we've seen throughout the pages of this book, Francis's spiritual journey always had freedom and perfect joy as its twin goals. He had attained freedom through his embrace of poverty, simplicity, and humility, and in finding freedom he also discovered joy. His final words, then, were also a praise offering to God for releasing him from the prison of ego and the dungeon of pride.

In thinking back over his life during his final moments, Francis must have realized that he had found freedom and perfect joy because in following Christ he discovered who he, Francis di Bernardone, really was. All the masks he'd donned at one time or another—the rich merchant's son, the youthful reveler, the would-be knight, the repairer of churches, even the founder of a religious order—all these were finally dropped, and he knew himself for what he most essentially was: a child of God, a being made in the likeness of the Creator, a spark of divine Love whose ultimate destiny is lovingly to affirm being. In thanking God for bringing him out of prison, then, Francis was also expressing his gratitude for the discovery and release of his own true self.

This is the destiny that each of us shares with Francis and with one another. We all have our own LaVernas. Once we arrive at them, we become who we really are, just as Francis did.

The masks drop away. We finally see ourselves as God's clear eye sees us.

The fourteenth-century mystic Meister Eckhart once exultantly told his congregation that he was more youthful as a middle-aged adult than he had been as a child, and that he fully expected to get younger and younger with each passing year. This is a startling thing to say, particularly when we realize that what Eckhart didn't mean was the platitudinous "you're as young as you feel" attitude so popular today. Eckhart's meaning was that his spiritual practice was gradually whittling away at the many false personae he'd superimposed on his true self, personae that prevented him from touching base with the Spirit of God dwelling in his soul.

The implication of his remark is that the goal of all humans ought to be growing younger each year until we return to the innocence, the purity, the spiritual transparency, with which we were born. Then we step out of the prison our own foolishness has locked us in. Then we regain our lost identity and, in so doing, regain God.

How different the world would be if we thought of life span in terms of "young-ing" rather than aging!

FOR REFLECTION

Have you made contact with who you really are, or are you still working your way through the many masks you wear?

MEDITATION

For Francis the decision to follow Christ allows him to become who he really is; and when he becomes who he really is, he is free. The ground of all our being is God, and in choosing to follow in the footsteps he left on creation, we rediscover the center from which our personal freedom derives. Only a true self can act freely, and we know that self only in the God who selves through us. In choosing God, we are choosing to be ourselves. God is the tie that binds us to ourselves; Christ is the face behind the masks we wear.

—Murray Bodo, *The Way of St. Francis*

CHAPTER THIRTY

~ Restoration ~

FRANCIS'S WORDS

God revealed a form of greeting to me, telling me that we should say, "God give you peace."

—*The Testament*

MIRROR

Above everything else Francis desired to depart and to be with Christ.

—Thomas of Celano, *First Life of Francis*

FRANCIS AND HIS FOLLOWERS INVENTED A NEW GREETING, ONE that startled some people when they first heard it. The greeting that Francis used whenever he met anyone on the road or in the field was "Peace." Most folks had never heard anyone say the word to them outside of Mass. In adopting it as his own special greeting, Francis clearly wanted to bring the holy love of the Eucharist into the world at large.

We've noted several times in these pages that many people seem to live sundered and hence unhappy lives. They're separated from God, from others, from their true selves, from what will make them genuinely joyful. This alienation, which St. Paul called "sin," exiles them into a bleak land of bondage and misery where it's impossible to become who they're meant to be. Healthy development flies out the window when our spiritual centers split apart or fragment. At best, all that can be hoped for is a minimalistic kind of existence in which we drag through each day as best we can.

Once we become who we are, once we can honestly thank God for releasing us from our prisons, we acquire the wondrous peace that Francis wished for everyone he met. Peace isn't merely the absence of violence, although that's how our war-weary age usually thinks of it. Above all, peace is restoration, the putting back together of what was broken. Peace is harmony, wholeness, stability, balance. Peace is the *integritas*, the internal unity, that the medieval philosophers argued was the hallmark of a spiritually healthy human being.

When we become who we're meant to be, we make peace with ourselves, with God, and with creation. We heal the fractures in reality caused by our earlier sundered lives, and we participate in the great work of cosmic restoration in which all things finally come to fruition in God. As good Francis showed us so many years ago, this harmony ripples across everything we do and everything we touch, manifesting itself in our thoughts, our words, our actions, and our own amphibious nature.

We pass on the peace of Christ, not just as a greeting but also as a deed. There can be no greater affirmation of being than this kind of restoration. There can be no more perfect joy than participation in this great "at-one-ment."

Let us follow Francis's example, then, by doing peace so that we and the entire universe might have peace.

Let us begin anew, for until now we have done little or nothing!

FOR REFLECTION

In what ways do you strive for restoration?

MEDITATION

However one may seek to explain it, the very essence of peace seems to be something that we absorb, something that comes like a gift in the very depth of our being. Again we may remember Christ's words: "Peace I leave with you, my peace I give unto you" [John 14:27, KJV].

—John Macquarrie, *The Concept of Peace*

SOURCES

INTRODUCTION

Thomas of Celano, *First Life*, in Marion A. Habig, ed., *Saint Francis of Assisi: Omnibus of Sources*, vol. 1 (Cincinnati: Franciscan Media, 2008), 329 (hereafter cited as *Omnibus* 1).

CHAPTER ONE

Omnibus 1, 80; Nikos Kazantzakis, *Saint Francis*, trans. P.A. Bien (Chicago: Loyola, 2005), 34; Leonardo Boff, *Saint Francis: A Model for Human Liberation* (New York: Crossroad, 1984), 131.

CHAPTER TWO

Omnibus 1, 98; Marion A. Habig, ed., *Saint Francis of Assisi, Omnibus of Sources*, vol. 2, (Cincinnati: Franciscan Media, 2008), 891 (hereafter cited as *Omnibus* 2); Georges Bernanos, *The Diary of a Country Priest*, trans. Pamela Morris (New York: Carroll and Graf, 2001), 2.

CHAPTER THREE

Francis of Assisi, vol. 2: *The Founder*, ed. Regis J. Armstrong, J.A. Wayne Hellman, and William J. Short (New York: New City, 2000), 245 (hereafter cited as *Francis of Assisi* 2); *Omnibus* 1, 365–366; C.S. Lewis, "The Weight of Glory," in *The Weight of Glory and Other Addresses*, ed. Walter Hooper (New York: Collier, 1962), 3–4.

CHAPTER FOUR

Omnibus 1, 95; *Omnibus* 1, 366.

Chapter Five

Omnibus 1, 67; Omnibus 1, 369–370; Gustavo Gutierrez, Essential Writings, ed. James B. Nickoloff (Minneapolis: Fortress), 154–155.

Chapter Six

Omnibus 1, 107; Omnibus 1, 640; Jean-Pierre de Caussade, Abandonment to Divine Providence, trans. John Beevers (New York: Image, 1975), 45.

Chapter Seven

Omnibus 1, 108; Omnibus 2, 907; Catherine de Hueck Doherty, Poustinia: Christian Spirituality of the East for Western Man (Combermere, Ontario: Madonna House, 1993), 38.

Chapter Eight

Omnibus 1, 106; Omnibus 1, 642–643; Carlo Carretto, I Sought and I Found, trans. Robert Barr (Maryknoll, NY: Orbis, 1985), 10. The "I want to be happy!" quotation is from Franco Zeffirelli's Brother Sun, Sister Moon (Los Angeles, CA: Paramont Pictures, 1972). The scene may be accessed at https://www.youtube.com/watch?v=Ev2d92_W47Y.

Chapter Nine

Omnibus 1, 118–19; Omnibus 2, 915; Charles de Foucauld, Writings, ed. Robert Ellsberg (Maryknoll, NY: Orbis, 1999), 70.

Chapter Ten

Francis of Assisi 2, 133; Kazantzakis, Saint Francis, 111. Plato, Phaedrus, trans. Walter Hamilton (New York: Penguin, 1973), 55–56.

CHAPTER ELEVEN

Omnibus 1, 133; *Omnibus* 2, 923; Omer Englebert, *St. Francis of Assisi: A Biography* (Cincinnati: Servant, 2013), 80.

CHAPTER TWELVE

Francis of Assisi 2, 147; *Omnibus* 1, 415; Thomas Merton, *The Wisdom of the Desert* (New York: New Directions, 1960), 63.

CHAPTER THIRTEEN

Omnibus 1, 471; *Omnibus* 1, 477; Leonard Foley, et al., *To Live as Francis Lived: A Guide for Secular Franciscans* (Cincinnati: St. Anthony Messenger Press, 2000), 71. Henri Nouwen writes of "downward mobility" in *The Selfless Way of Christ: Downward Mobility and the Spiritual Life* (Maryknoll, NY: Orbis, 2011).

CHAPTER FOURTEEN

Omnibus 1, 456; Julien Green, *God's Fool: The Life and Times of Francis of Assisi*, trans. Peter Heinegg (San Francisco: Harper and Row, 1983), 138; John Paul II, *Crossing the Threshold of Hope* (London: Jonathan Cape, 1994), 5. Dorothy Day writes about precarity in "Poverty and Precarity," in *Dorothy Day: Selected Writings*, ed. Robert Ellsberg (Maryknoll, NY: Orbis, 2005), 106–110.

CHAPTER FIFTEEN

Omnibus 1, 133; *Omnibus* 1, 698, 701; Andre Dupleix, *Fifteen Days of Prayer with Pierre Teilhard de Chardin*, trans. Victoria Hebert and Denis Sabourin (Liguori, MO: Liguori, 1999), 32.

CHAPTER SIXTEEN

Omnibus 1, 81; *Omnibus* 2, 1501–1502; Carlo Carretto, *I, Francis*, trans. Robert R. Barr (Maryknoll, NY: Orbis, 2000), 52.

CHAPTER SEVENTEEN

Francis of Assisi 2, 124; *Omnibus* 1, 665; *The Simone Weil Reader*, ed. George A. Panichas (New York: David McKay, 1977), 107.

CHAPTER EIGHTEEN

Omnibus 1, 467; William Shakespeare, *Merchant of Venice*, act 5, scene 1.

CHAPTER NINETEEN

Omnibus 2, 942–943; *Omnibus* 1, 436–437; The George MacDonald quotation is found in C.S. Lewis, *Surprised by Joy* (New York: Harcourt, Brace, Jovanovich, 1966), 210.

CHAPTER TWENTY

Omnibus 1, 131; Green, *God's Fool*, 159; Angela of Foligno, *Complete Works*, trans. Paul LaChance (Mahwah, NJ: Paulist, 1993), 170.

CHAPTER TWENTY-ONE

Omnibus 1, 50; *The Little Flowers of Saint Francis*, trans. Raphael Brown (New York: Image, 1958), 43; Blaise Pascal, *Pensees*, trans. A.J. Krailsheimer (New York: Penguin, 1966), 309.

CHAPTER TWENTY-TWO

Omnibus 2, 1155; *Omnibus* 2, 904.

CHAPTER TWENTY-THREE

Omnibus 1, 443–444; *Omnibus* 1, 440–441; Henri Nouwen, *The Living Reminder* (San Francisco: Harper, 1998), 51–52.

CHAPTER TWENTY-FOUR

Omnibus, 1, 81; *Omnibus* 1, 712–713.

CHAPTER TWENTY-FIVE

Omnibus 1, 322; *Omnibus* 1, 319; *Little Flowers*, 251.

CHAPTER TWENTY-SIX

Omnibus 1, 318; *Omnibus* 1, 318; Kent Nerburn, *Make Me an Instrument of Your Peace* (San Francisco: Harper, 1999), 87.

CHAPTER TWENTY-SEVEN

The Little Flowers, 190; *Omnibus* 2, 953; Rufus Jones, *The Luminous Trail* (New York: Macmillan, 1949), 77–78.

CHAPTER TWENTY-EIGHT

Francis of Assisi 2, 164; *Omnibus* 2, 996; William J. Short, *Poverty and Joy: The Franciscan Tradition* (Maryknoll, NY: Orbis, 1999), 127.

CHAPTER TWENTY-NINE

Omnibus 1, 84; Murray Bodo, *The Way of St. Francis* (Cincinnati: Franciscan Media, 1995), 118–119.

CHAPTER THIRTY

Omnibus 1, 68; *Omnibus* 1, 288; John Macquarrie, *The Concept of Peace* (London: SCM, 1973), 65.

ACKNOWLEDGMENTS

Many thanks to the team at Franciscan Media, and especially to Mary Carol Kendzia and editorial director Jon Sweeney. Jon knows more about St. Francis than most, and his counsel on this new edition of *Perfect Joy* was invaluable.

ABOUT THE AUTHOR

Kerry Walters is a professor of philosophy and peace and justice studies at Gettysburg College in Pennsylvania. He is a prolific author whose recent books include *Giving Up god to Find God: Breaking Free of Idolatry; John Paul II: A Short Biography; John XXIII: A Short Biography;* and *Junipero Serra: A Short Biography.*